COCOMANIA

COCOMANIA

**How Coco Gauff Won the US Open and Became
America's Next Great Tennis Superstar**

DAN WOLKEN

Post Hill
PRESS

A POST HILL PRESS BOOK
ISBN: 979-8-88845-499-2
ISBN (eBook): 979-8-88845-500-5

Cocomania:
How Coco Gauff Won the US Open and Became America's Next Great Tennis
Superstar
© 2024 by Post Hill Press
All Rights Reserved

Cover design by Cody Corcoran

This is a work of nonfiction. All people, locations, events, and situations are portrayed to the best of the author's memory.

Post Hill Press
New York • Nashville
posthillpress.com

Published in the United States of America
1 2 3 4 5 6 7 8 9 10

CONTENTS

CHAPTER 1

Every seat in Arthur Ashe Stadium was full, and the roar of nearly twenty-four thousand people was building. Coco Gauff knew she was about to win the US Open if she could just keep it together for a few more minutes.

She told herself not to envision holding the trophy, or what she might say to the crowd, or what emotions might come over her when she saw her mom and dad. The truth is, Coco had thought about this moment since she was eight years old, watching this very tournament from the upper deck at Arthur Ashe Stadium. She had worked her entire life for this opportunity, and she wasn't going to let it go. But she had also suffered enough heartbreaks as a tennis player to know those thoughts weren't going to help her now that she was just four points from the championship.

"I told myself to get it out of my head," she said. "I was just trying my best to just focus on the point ahead of me."[1]

Coco had come nearly to the end of a brilliant match against Aryna Sabalenka, the new number-one player in the world, but it hadn't been easy.

Aryna is the most powerful player in the sport, launching shots that can speed by you in the blink of an eye. When she's on her game, she's almost unbeatable. But her style of play, hitting almost every ball as hard as she can, is risky.

At the beginning of the US Open final, it looked like one of those days where everything was going Aryna's way. But in women's tennis, it takes two sets to win a match. So even though Coco lost the first set 6–2, she still had a chance to turn things around. Coco isn't just a great player: she's a problem-solver, and she became very good at it during this tournament in particular. Her confidence in those tough moments seemed unshakeable. If she could just hang around long enough to make Aryna question herself or get nervous, maybe things could turn in a different direction.

But immediately after the first set, Coco was suddenly the more nervous of the two. All those people had come to cheer her to victory, and she was as worried about letting them down as she was about letting herself down. With so much at stake, Coco went to the bathroom after the first set, threw some water on her face, and reminded herself she had to keep fighting.

"I've got to just reset and redo it," she said.[2]

For the next hour and twenty-five minutes, Coco did exactly that. She didn't think about what had already happened and instead focused on staying positive and running as fast as she could for every ball. At that moment, it didn't need to be pretty. This was the biggest match of her career, and Coco's best chance to win was simply to make Aryna hit as many shots as possible.

With her style of play, more shots meant more opportunities to feel the pressure and more chances to miss.

Little by little, Coco's plan began to work. Aryna started to look a little confused, unsure what to do as Coco raced around the court like a golden retriever chasing a toy.

Finally, the in fourth game of the second set, the misses started to come off Aryna's racket. Coco started to get more comfortable; with every point she won, the crowd got louder and louder until the match was all even and headed to a deciding third set.

"Be physical now, be physical!" Coco's coach, Brad Gilbert, kept shouting from the stands.

By the third set, Aryna knew this was becoming Coco's match and that the title was slipping away. She wasn't just trying to beat a great opponent and a crowd that wanted her to lose, but she was also fighting herself.

"Sometimes I can get emotional," she said. "On the court, I was overthinking and missing—not easy balls— but balls I shouldn't be missing."[3]

All of those misses started to add up as Coco raced out to a 3–0 lead, then a 4–0 lead in the deciding set. Aryna steadied herself to get back to 4–2, hoping that maybe she could make it close enough for Coco's nerves to kick in once again. But when Coco smacked a forehand into the open court that gave her a 5–2 lead in the third set, their body language couldn't have been more different. As the crowd erupted, Coco raised her left fist and calmly walked to her chair. Aryna just looked at the ground.

For a player one game away from the title, that sixty-second rest break as the players change ends can be excruciating. Roger Federer, one of the greatest players of all time, described the tension he felt playing in the most important matches and the biggest tournaments in the world as his head being flooded with a million ideas. It's a natural thing, even for someone who has won every big trophy imaginable.

"Sometimes it slows down your legs, your pulse starts racing…that can stress you out a tad," he said. "I always say I'm happy I feel that way because it means I care."[4]

In those moments, players usually try to slow down their breathing and focus on anything other than winning the match. Because in tennis, unlike basketball or football, you can't run out the clock if you have the lead. The only way to take home the tournament is to win the last game, and the only way to win the last game is to win four points. You have to keep your focus all the way to the end.

So when it was time for Coco to serve what she hoped would be the final game of the match, she took her stance and bounced the ball eight times. She delivered her first serve and rallied with Aryna, moving right to left, then back to the right again before Aryna tried to crush a forehand as hard as she could. But she hit it too far, about a foot beyond the baseline!

One down, three to go.

On the next point, Aryna tried something different—a drop shot that she meant to barely float over the net and land softly, hoping to catch Coco by surprise. Once Coco recognized what was coming, she sprinted forward and clenched her left fist for just a moment when Aryna's shot landed in the net. Two points away!

As she got closer to the finish line, Coco quickly let go of her emotions. She didn't scream or celebrate. She didn't smile. She was as locked into the job as she'd ever been. After just a few seconds, she was right back on the baseline, ready to serve again.

This time, it was a long rally. They went back and forth and back and forth, pushing each other around the court until Coco slightly mishit a ball that shot way up into the air and landed short on the other side of the net. For Aryna, this was an easy shot, one she had probably practiced tens of thousands of times during her life. So she scooted into position, took the racket back, and got ready to smash it for a winner—only this time it wasn't a winner. She had pulled it wide!

This was it. Everything Coco had dreamed of since she started focusing on tennis at age seven was just one point away from becoming reality.

The fans came to their feet and started to take out their cell phones, hoping to capture the scene. In just a few seconds, it had become the loudest, happiest place in all of New York, bursting in celebration at what was about to happen. Coco paced around the court for a few seconds and took one deep breath as she stepped up to the base-line, as focused as she could be in that moment.

Then she started bouncing the ball, rocking back into her serving motion for what she hoped would be the point that would make her a US Open champion.

***

To understand the importance of that moment for Coco, let's talk about how tennis works. In a normal year, a professional player will enter around twenty tournaments across the globe, each one presenting a unique challenge. There are different surfaces, different balls, different weather, and different pressures waiting for players as they hop from country to country, often spending months at a time away from their friends and families.

On one hand, it's a glamorous life, playing every week in a new place and spending time in some of the world's most exciting cities. On the other hand, it's a constant routine of packing up suitcases, rushing through airports, eating meals on the go, and having to organize practice time or medical treatment in unfamiliar places. There's not much time to celebrate wins or be sad about losses because the next tournament is always just around the corner.

Maybe the best way to describe it came from Coco's doubles partner and one of her best friends on the tour, Jessie Pegula. She lost her final set 6–0 at a tournament in Qatar—tennis players call it "eating a bagel" because that's exactly what the zero looks like—and posted a selfie with a bag of tortilla chips on social media:

> *Everyone: "What is it like playing on tour? It must be so amazing!"*
>
> *Me: gets bageled on your birthday, sitting eating Doritos at midnight, waiting to get on a 16 hr flight home. (Crying/laughing emoji)*

But players put up with those hardships and the endless travel/practice/tournament cycle because they want to win one of the four biggest events on the tour, which are collectively called the Grand Slam.

The first one is in January at the Australian Open, which is like the start of a new season. Everybody is fresh and happy and excited to be in the warm weather Down Under while it's winter back home for players from Europe and North America.

The French Open takes place at the height of spring in Paris and is played on clay, which looks like a court covered in red dirt. It's actually made up of crushed bricks and produces a high bounce that some players find easier to deal with than others.

Just a few weeks after the French Open, the game changes again at Wimbledon, which is played at a private club in London on courts made of grass. This is closer to the way tennis was played originally in the 1870s, when it started to spread all around the world.

Though players no longer use small, heavy wooden rackets or wear long pants and formal dresses to play tennis like they did back then, Wimbledon tries to preserve as much tradition as possible and is considered the most important tournament of the year. But because grass courts are so rare now—they're very difficult and expensive to maintain—even the top professionals don't have much experience playing on them. Some players can handle the weird bounces they get on grass courts and the unique movements it takes to prevent from slipping, but for others it's like trying to play on a sheet of ice.

"Grass is for cows," said Ivan Lendl, a great champion who won eight Grand Slam titles but never Wimbledon, losing twice in the finals.

After that, the action shifts to the US Open, which is the favorite time of year for most American players like Coco because of the familiar surroundings and the crowd support they get playing in their home country.

Winning any of those four tournaments launches a tennis player's career to a different level, and in some ways changes their whole life. Sure, a Grand Slam title comes with a nice trophy and a big paycheck, but the most important part of it is making history and putting your name alongside the best who have ever played the sport.

Ever since she was a little girl, Coco had seen herself in that group, holding those trophies and posing for pictures under a storm of confetti just like Venus and Serena Williams, the two players she idolized the most. Even at twelve years old, when she won her age group at the prestigious Junior Orange Bowl tournament, Coco confidently declared: "I want to be the greatest of all time."[5]

Coco had expected to win Grand Slams at an early age because that's what Serena and Venus had done. The entire tennis world expected it, too, after fifteen-year-old Coco beat Venus in the first round of Wimbledon in 2019. That was the first time most people saw Coco play, and even though Venus was thirty-nine years old and had not been at the top of the sport for quite a while, it was eye-opening to see someone so young play with so much poise on such a big stage.

"I think the sky's the limit, it really is," Venus said after the match.[6]

But as talented as she was, Coco wasn't a fully developed player who knew what she wanted to do on the court all the time. That's completely natural for somebody so young playing against older, more experienced professionals. But when the Grand Slam titles weren't coming right away, or when she couldn't match certain milestones like Serena winning her first Grand Slam at age seventeen, Coco started to ask herself if something was wrong.

"I felt like I had a time limit on when I should win one, and if I won one after a certain age it wouldn't be an achievement," she said.[7]

By her nineteenth birthday, though, Coco was no longer making those comparisons. She had established herself as one of the ten best players in the world, which is a remarkable thing when you consider how many millions of girls around the world play tennis and hope to one day be on the tour. But when she played some of the other top-ranked women like Aryna, and especially her biggest nemesis, Iga Świątek, she was losing more often than she was winning. Some critics were questioning whether she was ever going to be good enough to take home one of those big, shiny Grand Slam trophies.

But Coco had to accept that she was on a different path, and it was going to be filled with ups and downs. The bottom line was that focusing on records like Serena's twenty-three Grand Slam titles or winning a certain tournament wasn't helping her become a better player. She just had to have faith that if she did the right things in practice and kept improving, all her dreams would eventually come true.

***

For a few weeks before the US Open, it started to feel like Coco's time was coming. Her preparation since coming back to North America for the summer hard court season had been almost perfect, with just one close loss to her friend and doubles partner Jessie in the quarterfinals of a tournament in Canada.

Everything started to click for Coco in Washington, D.C., where she even surprised herself by winning four straight matches without losing a set. After the loss to Jessie, she moved on to Cincinnati, where she had to face Iga in the semifinals. At the time, Iga had been ranked number one for more than a year and already won four Grand Slams in her career, including the 2022 US Open. It had been a difficult matchup for Coco in the past, with Iga winning all seven of their meetings and none of them being particularly close.

But for this match, Coco's mindset was different. For the previous few weeks, her coaches had been telling her to focus on serving with more power and taking more risk. Iga was the perfect opponent to see if that strategy would work.

Unlike every other shot in tennis, where you have to react to what your opponent does, the serve is totally under your control. That's why the player who has an easier time winning their service games, or "holding serve," will usually win the match.

Think of it this way: If you are a great server, you'll win a lot of points with just one or two shots because the returner doesn't have enough time to hit the ball exactly where they want. They're just trying to get it back in the court, which is a big advantage for the server.

On the other hand, players who struggle to serve have to work a lot harder because the returner can pick any shot they want. Tennis is a game of anticipation and reacting quickly when things don't go according to plan. When the server doesn't know where the ball is coming back, the game becomes much more difficult and they'll lose their service games—which is called "getting broken"—more often.

That's especially true against a player like Iga, who likes to pounce on a weak serve and immediately gain the upper hand in a rally. Once Iga lures opponents into her spiderweb, moving opponents from side to side until she has opened up enough room on the court to hit an easy winner, it's almost impossible to get out. If Coco wanted to win this time, she couldn't allow herself to get drawn into that trap. Holding serve, and doing it easily, would be the key to victory.

"In the past she's broken me, like fairly easy pretty much every match," Coco said. "I knew maybe my typical safe serve wasn't going to work today. So I was just trying to be aggressive."[8]

In the end, Coco did exactly what she wanted to do. Though it was a long, difficult battle over two hours, fifty minutes, Coco served brilliantly and won more of the important points that could have swung the match in either direction. When she emerged as the 7–6, 3–6, 6–4 winner, she pounded her chest and lead out two huge screams before coming to the net to shake Iga's hand.

In that moment, it was the most important win of Coco's life not just because it was the first time she had beaten Iga, but because she had proven to herself that she was ready to compete at the highest level just in time for the final Grand Slam of the year. The US Open was just a couple weeks away, and Coco was heading to New York as the player everyone had their eyes on.

CHAPTER 2

The US Open isn't just a Grand Slam tournament: it's a spectacle that takes place every year in Queens, New York, just a 45-minute subway ride from the bright lights and 24/7 energy of Times Square.

In the beginning, America's biggest tennis tournament was called the U.S. National Championship, and it was only for men. A handful of years later, in 1887, the first women's event was held at a country club near Philadelphia.

Starting in 1915, and for most of the next sixty-two years, the tournament was played on the grass courts at West Side Tennis Club, about a fifteen-minute drive from the current US Open site. But as tennis became more popular, the United States Tennis Association decided that its showcase tournament had outgrown its surroundings and needed a huge complex with enough room for tens of thousands of people to come watch every day.

So in 1978, the US Open moved just down the road to a piece of land inside a public park. Unlike Wimbledon, which is played at a private club for the rich and famous in England, the national tennis center would be a place anyone could play for most of the year—except, of course, during the two weeks of the US Open.

Over time, the site grew to include Arthur Ashe Stadium, the largest tennis arena in the world with nearly twenty-four thousand seats, as well as fourteen thousand–seat Louis Armstrong Stadium and several other courts where thousands of people can watch tennis from 11 a.m. until late at night.

But what truly makes the US Open different is the atmosphere and the constant buzz of activity coming from New York City. At most tournaments, tennis is played in quiet surroundings with fans who cheer politely. The US Open feels more chaotic, like an NFL or NBA game, where fans are noisy and rowdy and sometimes even a bit rude when they aren't getting the result they want. It's not an environment every player enjoys.

"I think the US Open just doesn't suit my personality," said Petra Kvitová, a player from the Czech Republic who won Wimbledon twice but never made it past the quarterfinals in New York. "I'm more of a calm person. There, it's noisy all day, cars are everywhere and it takes so long to get to the site. I know that those things shouldn't matter when you're playing, but I just find they drain your energy."[9]

For American players, though, it's a much more favorable situation because the crowds shower them with support. It can be a lot of pressure to play in front of your home fans, but it's also an opportunity that comes around only once a year.

"Being an American playing at the US Open is incredible,"[10] said Sloane Stephens, who won the title in 2017. "I think this atmosphere, out of all the Slams, is pretty unmatched. I think this is like the peak of the peak."

After her run to the title in Cincinnati, there was no doubt that Coco was coming into the 2023 US Open as the main attraction, her face splashed on ads and billboards across the city. This represented a huge change in tennis. For many years, Roger Federer and Serena Williams were the two stars that fans wanted tickets to watch and all the big celebrities came out to support. But both of them retired in 2022, and American fans were starving for a new player to get behind. Coco seemed to be next in line.

But this was also new territory for her. Though it was Coco's seventeenth time to play in a Grand Slam, and she had lived so much of her life playing under big expectations, she had never before been considered one of the top contenders to win the title. Before the tournament, Coco tried to downplay how far she might go.

"I'm really just enjoying the process of having a tennis career and the ups and downs," she said. "I know I'm up right now, and I know I'm going to experience a down. Hopefully not this week, but it could happen. I know it's going to happen. It's impossible to stay up all the time."[11]

Though her confidence and her game were at all-time highs, Coco didn't want to look too far ahead. She had enough experience to know how difficult it is to survive seven consecutive matches against top opponents at this tournament, and she couldn't take anyone for granted— even her first-round opponent, Laura Siegemund.

But when the tournament bracket came out, that wasn't the match the media was talking about. Instead, it looked like Coco was on a collision course once again to play Iga, the number-one seed, in the quarterfinals. Not everybody on Coco's team was thrilled about that possibility so early in the tournament.

"I was thinking, 'Oh, it might be better if she was in the opposite half,'" Coco's coach, Brad Gilbert, said. "But you never know."

There was a lot of work to be done by both of them before that match was even possible.

***

The first day of the US Open is always buzzing with anticipation, and it's a huge honor for a player to be assigned one of the two night matches on Ashe Stadium. It was even more special in 2023, as the U.S. Tennis Association was celebrating its fiftieth anniversary of giving men and women equal prize money.

Though women's sports have come a long way toward being accepted and celebrated, it wasn't always that way. For a long time, women and young girls who aspired to be athletes didn't have professional sports leagues or college opportunities and could only play as a hobby. Tennis was one of the first to recognize that women could play just as exciting a game as the men and draw big audiences to stadiums around the world. It didn't come easily, though.

In 1970, just as tennis was beginning to expand into a real professional sport where players competed for money and not just trophies, nine women got together and decided to start their own tour. The most important of those players was Billie Jean King, who had been number one in the world and believed that women deserved more than the small amounts of money they were being offered at most tournaments.

In 1972, Billie Jean King got a $10,000 check for winning the US Open—less than half of what men's champion Ilie Năstase earned—even though she had seen surveys showing that many women's players were just as popular if not more than the men. After the tournament, she threatened not to play the next year if the prize money wasn't equal. The U.S. Tennis Association said it would need help to make that happen, so Billie Jean convinced a deodorant company to make up the difference through a sponsorship agreement.

Over time, the other Grand Slams followed the US Open's lead, though it took until 2007 for Wimbledon to get on board. But thanks to the efforts of Billie Jean and many others throughout history, the top women's players became some of the most highly paid athletes in world. In 2023, the US Open winner was set to receive $3 million.

Even all these years later, the concept of equal pay has its detractors. Some critics argue that because the women play best-of-three sets while men play best-of-five at the Grand Slams, the men deserve a larger share of the money.

Others will say, without evidence, that men's matches are more popular so they should be paid more.

The truth isn't so simple. Part of what has put women's tennis on an equal plane with the men is that each generation of stars has inspired the next one to be even greater. From Chris Evert and Martina Navratilova to Steffi Graf and Monica Seles to the Williams sisters, there is a straight line to players like Coco who empower young girls to play sports and show young boys that it's cool to root for women. There are even some years where more Americans watch the women's US Open final on television than watch the men.

In 2022, when Serena Williams announced that the US Open would be her final tournament, tickets for Arthur Ashe Stadium sold out almost instantly. After she had thrilled fans for more than twenty years, everyone wanted to be there to say goodbye to the "GOAT"—the greatest of all time. Unfortunately, Serena had been struggling with injuries for a couple years. She wasn't a contender to win the tournament, but on her best day she could still beat anyone.

In the second round, Serena faced Annet Kontaveit, who was ranked number two in the world. But in the third set, Serena did what the great champions do. She found a way to turn the clock back and play the kind of powerful, precise tennis that won her twenty-three Grand Slam titles. After winning 7–6, 2–6, 6–2, Serena was onto the third round. With some upsets taking out a lot of the top-ranked players, it looked like she might have a chance to make it into the second week of the tournament.

But Serena's run ended a couple days later against Ajla Tomljanović, who played the best match of her career to win in three sets. It was a valiant effort from Serena, who had opportunities to win the match but faded just a little bit toward the end despite having one of the loudest tennis crowds ever cheering her on.

Though it was a disappointing night, it wasn't a sad one. Everyone had witnessed a wonderful competition and a historic moment in sports. After match point, Serena took the microphone to thank the crowd and her parents, Richard and Oracene, who focused their entire lives on giving Venus and Serena a chance to become great tennis players.

"It all started with my parents, and they deserve everything, so I'm really grateful for them," Serena said.

When Venus and Serena were growing up, their family was ridiculed because Richard had not played tennis himself and yet was out on the public courts in Compton, California, trying to coach his daughters to be champions. And as a Black family in a sport that was predominantly played at country clubs for wealthy and mostly white people, the Williamses faced plenty of discrimination and doubters along the way.

When Coco began to show a talent for playing tennis at age six, her father Corey began to study how all kinds of champions were formed. How they trained, what tournaments they played as youngsters, how they progressed to become pros. He was especially interested in Richard Williams. Though he did not play the sport at a high level and didn't have a coaching background, Richard had a deep belief both in his daughters and in his own ability to get them to the top. Though Coco had several coaches who helped out from time to time, Corey was the one in charge, taking his daughter to the courts for hours on the weekends to feed her balls and teach proper technique.

In some ways, Corey was trying to copy the same plan Richard Williams laid out when his daughters were little. He had a vision of Coco becoming a pro by the time she was eighteen and formed a plan—patterned after Serena and Venus—to make it a reality.

"If it wasn't for the Williams sisters, Coco would not be a tennis player," Coco's mom, Candi, said.[12]

When Coco was eight, her family realized that she not only had a lot of talent, but also a competitive intensity and love for the sport that was unusual for someone her age. But they also realized that the best training and competition was in Florida, not the suburbs of Atlanta where the family lived and worked.

At that point, they made a decision to move the family, including Coco's two younger brothers, to Delray Beach, where their entire lives would revolve around Coco's tennis. Corey would be her full-time coach, and it was Candi's job to make sure she was getting an education through homeschooling programs. They tried to give Coco a normal life—as normal as possible, anyway, with tennis taking up so much time. Just like with the Williams sisters, everything was geared around practice.

They wanted to give Coco the best chance to become a great player.

***

At the 2022 US Open, Serena was on her way out and Coco was on her way up, possibly to becoming the biggest star in women's tennis. The entire world wanted to see them play each other at least once before Serena retired, but for one reason or another it just wasn't in the cards. The only possibility remaining was a matchup in the US Open semifinals, but that was a long way away. Both would have to win five matches, which is something Coco had only done once before at a Grand Slam.

When Serena lost, Coco was a bit sad that the opportunity to play each other was never going to happen. Given how much she had copied from her idol and how much she looked up to her, Coco said it was going to be the biggest regret of her career.

"Before Serena came along, there was not really an icon of the sport that looked like me," Coco said. "So growing up, I never thought that I was different because the number-one player in the world was somebody who looked like me."[13]

With Serena out of the tournament, the focus shifted to whether this might be the time for Coco to take her place at the top of the sport. The expectations began to build as Coco rolled through her first four matches without dropping a set. The fans that had been hoping for a Serena run to the title began to get behind Coco in a big way. At every one of her matches, chants of "Co-co! Co-co!" rang out through Arthur Ashe Stadium, and she was responding with great tennis to reach the quarterfinals.

"This is a surreal moment for me," she said.

Everything looked set up for Coco to go further, maybe even all the way to the finals. She had beaten her next opponent, Caroline Garcia, in both of their previous meetings.

But tennis is a sport with small margins between winning and losing, especially at that stage of the tournament. And Garcia had been on the biggest hot streak of her life for several weeks, so in a way Coco wasn't even playing the same opponent she had beaten before.

When they faced each other on Arthur Ashe Stadium, it wasn't Coco's best day. Maybe it was the pressure finally getting to her, or maybe it was just Caroline continuing to play terrific tennis, but Coco made too many errors and lost convincingly, 6–3, 6–4.

Coco was disappointed not to make the semis, but she was proud of how well she competed. It was only her fourth U.S. Open, and it was the first time she had ever made it to the second week. Though Coco still hadn't reached her goals of winning Grand Slams and becoming number one in the world, the 2022 season felt like progress. She was more a consistent player and a smarter player, but she also knew she would enter 2023 with a different spotlight on her.

With Serena out of the game, the tennis world was looking for the next superstar to take her place. At the next U.S. Open, which was going to be a celebration of women's tennis and fifty years of equality, all eyes were going to be on Coco.

"Sometimes being a woman, a Black woman in the world, you kind of settle for less," she said. "I feel like Serena taught me that, from watching her. She never settled for less. I can't remember a moment in her career or life that she settled for less."[14]

It was a lesson Coco would have to keep reminding herself of for most of the next year.

CHAPTER 3

At the start of Wimbledon began in 2019, you would have had to be one of the biggest tennis experts in the world to know anything about Coco Gauff. But just a few days into the tournament, the back page of the *Daily Mail*—one of London's biggest newspapers—said it all: "We've gone loco over Coco!"

To even get into a Grand Slam like Wimbledon, you either have to be ranked close to the top one hundred in the world or win three matches in the qualifying rounds, which is basically a tournament just to get into the main tournament. At just fifteen years old, with very few professional matches under her belt, Coco wasn't even ranked high enough to get into qualifying. But because she had earned a reputation as one of the top junior players in the world and had done well in some low-level pro tournaments, Wimbledon invited her to compete as a wild-card entry to see if she could earn her way into the main tournament.

Coco won all three of her qualifying matches easily, becoming the youngest player to get into Wimbledon since professionals were first allowed to play in 1968. That fact alone got the media's attention: Who was this young girl with a bright smile that seemed permanently affixed to her face? Where was she from? How good was she already, and what kind of potential did she have in the future?

A handful of media reporters followed Coco off the court after she qualified and asked her a few questions. Among them was who she'd like to play in the first round. Naturally, Coco said she wanted to play Venus or Serena Williams.

"It would be a dream come true," she said.

The tournament brackets are chosen by a random draw, so the odds of facing one of the Williams sisters were pretty low. But somehow, almost as if fate intervened, Coco got what she wanted: a matchup with Venus.

The storylines were almost too good to be true. Venus was thirty-nine years old and nearing the end of her career. But it didn't seem so long ago that she was the up-and-coming prodigy, playing her first professional match at age fourteen while her father Richard claimed that she was going to become the best in the world.

When Venus won Wimbledon for the first time in 2000, the Williams family from Compton, California, had conquered tennis' most exclusive club. Venus would go on to win the singles championship four more times, while Serena took home seven titles. Remarkably, they played each other four times in the final and won the Wimbledon doubles together on six occasions.

But perhaps Venus' most important contribution to the tournament's history came in her fight for equal pay.

Unlike the US Open, which began paying the same prize money to men and women starting in 1973, Wimbledon continued to pay men's players more for decades. Venus used her platform as the tournament's champion to argue for the club to change its policy, even writing an essay in 2006 that appeared in one of England's most important newspapers. In it, Venus said that Wimbledon had sent the message that she was a "second-class champion"[15] by paying her less, and that the club would look silly in the future for not respecting men and women equally.

The essay caught the attention of politicians, who began pressuring the club to change its ways. One year later, Wimbledon gave in and became the final Grand

Slam tournament to award equal prize money. Venus considers it one of the biggest achievements in her career.

"I'd like to think that my decision to stand up for what's right resonated with the right people," she wrote in another essay in 2023. "Before that time, I didn't envision myself as an activist. Things just tend to happen in your life, and when you find yourself in a position to make a difference, you need to be bold enough to take the lead."[16]

Even from a young age, Coco was mindful of how much the players who came before her contributed to making women's tennis a premiere sport around the world. She was particularly in awe of Venus and Serena, without whom she may not have ever shown an interest in tennis.

Now Coco was on the same path to stardom, although it was a long way before she could even think about having the kind of career the Williams sisters had. It was already going to be special to play in her first Grand Slam. Getting to do it against Venus was like a fairy tale come to life.

No matter what happened, there wasn't going to be any shame or disappointment if the hype was a little too much for Coco. Venus, after all, had lost her first-ever Wimbledon match when she was seventeen. Three years later, she was the champion. Coco had plenty of time.

"She's a great girl," Serena said before the tournament began. "I love her dad. They're just really cool people. It's a great moment for her and for Venus."[17]

Make no mistake, though: Venus expected to win. In all honesty, that's what Coco expected, too.

Wimbledon is the most historic tournament in the world, and it's rare for anyone to have success the first time they play on the famous grass courts of the All England Club. As much as Coco believed in herself, beating Venus on that occasion seemed like a really tall task.

But no matter what happened, it was also going to be a learning experience. For the first time in her life, she would get to feel what it was like to be on one of the big courts at a Grand Slam with millions of people watching.

***

When Coco first walked out onto Court 1 for the warm-up, it was bigger than it had seemed during practice. Maybe it was the sight of all the people sitting in the seats for the first time, or maybe it was just being nervous about playing a tournament and an opponent she had watched growing up.

Coco put on her headphones and tried to lose herself in the music blaring in her ears. It seemed to calm her down a little bit.

But then, as it came time to play the first point, everything got quiet except for the voice of the chair umpire:

"First set. Venus Williams to serve. Ready. Play."

With those words, Coco's first-ever Grand Slam match was underway. As she got ready to return serve, she hopped around the baseline, moving her feet in tandem from left to right and back again. Then she leaned forward, swaying back and forth to keep her body agile and ready to launch in any direction depending on the trajectory of the ball.

And then, as Venus delivered a serve into Coco's backhand that didn't require her to move at all, she weakly hit it into the net and put her left hand over her face.

If there were any remaining nerves, though, they went away quickly because it was clear that Coco could play at the same level as the five-time champion. If anything, after Coco broke serve for a 3–2 lead in the first set, it was Venus who started to look little bit anxious on the court. Coco wasn't just playing solid tennis; her speed around the court was giving Venus a lot to think about. It was difficult for Venus to get a shot past Coco, and the more she tried, the more she missed.

"C'monnnnnnn!" Coco shouted as Venus hit a backhand into the net to finish the first set, 6–4.

The second set was more of the same. Just like earlier in the match, Coco broke serve for a 3–2 lead and looked like she had total control. Venus was running out of time and didn't seem to have many answers for the way Coco was playing.

But then, right when the finish line came into view, there was a wobble. Coco came out for her service game at 4–3, sent her first serve long and her second into the net. On the next point, she got her second serve in, but Venus' return took a strange sideways hop and threw off Coco's rhythm. Her miss gave Venus a 0–30 lead and chance to get right back in the match. Another double fault by Coco on 30–40 had given Venus new life. Few things in tennis are harder than finishing matches, especially against a legend, and it looked like Coco might finally be feeling the importance of the moment.

"I wasn't really nervous," she said. "I was just going for my serve. I'm playing against one of the greatest players of all time. You never know what to expect from them. I was just like, 'Get the serve in the court next time.'"[18]

These are the moments in tennis where you learn about a player's mentality. Once they've let something slip away, do they get tense? Do they play safer? Do they take more risk? Can they get past the mistake they just made and start to execute again? Nobody knew how Coco would handle it because she'd never played in a match like this or against an opponent like Venus.

At 4–4 and deuce, both players faced maybe the biggest point of the match. Coco seemed like she wanted to keep the ball in the middle of the court and make it a long point. Venus wanted to move Coco from side to side and create space to hit a winner. But the point changed when Coco ran to the corner for a little backhand flick that caught Venus slightly by surprise as she was moving forward to the net. Venus' only play was to let it bounce, but she couldn't get any power on the shot and it sailed high over the net with enough hang time for Coco to sprint up to the ball and slam it as hard as she could to win the point. A few moments later, Coco had broken serve again and was on the verge of beating one of the most decorated players of all time.

"There was so much drama going on," she said. [19]

In the end, Coco handled it like she'd been through dozens of matches like this. Even though the final game was tense, with Venus somehow staying alive after three match points, Coco was able to keep the ball in the court just enough to get one final missed forehand from her opponent. When Venus' final shot went into the net, Coco dropped her racket on the ground and put both hands on top of her head. When she made her way to the net, tears beginning to fill her eyes, a smiling Venus awaited her for the handshake. All Coco could think to say was to thank her for everything she'd done for women's tennis.

"I met her before, but I didn't really have the guts to say anything," Coco said. "I mean, now or ever."[20]

It was just one win of what she hoped would be many, but this one was going to be unlike any match Coco had played before or would ever play again. Though she had been destined to become a superstar from the time she was a little girl, nearly everything in Coco's life was about to change in the blink of an eye.

At just fifteen years old, she had arrived.

***

The win over Venus turned Coco into a sensation all across the world. Though tennis had known many teenage prodigies over the years, nobody had made this big of a splash in the era of social media. Immediately after the Venus match, Coco was pumped to learn that her Instagram account had crossed forty thousand followers.

But that was just the beginning.

Suddenly, everyone wanted a piece of Coco. The media was fascinated by someone so young who played such mature tennis on the world's biggest stage. Companies saw her potential as a marketing giant and wanted to put their logos on her outfit. Fans were clamoring for tickets to her next match. Every single player, man or woman, was asked about Coco in their press conferences.

"I think it was an amazing situation, to play somebody twenty-three or twenty-four years older. That stuff doesn't happen every day," said Roger Federer, the eight-time Wimbledon champion. "I thought it was super special for Coco. I thought she handled it great. She wanted to be on the big court. She wanted to play against her idol. That's where good players shine."[21]

The hype only grew as Coco scored a routine 6–3, 6–3 victory over Magdaléna Rybáriková in the second round. By her third match against Polona Hercog, Coco was such a big draw that Wimbledon organizers put her in the prime slot on Centre Court. For someone who had never played at a Grand Slam before, it was quite a rush.

"I wasn't expecting any of this," she said. "A lot of celebrities were DMing, posting at me. I'm kind of star-struck. It's been hard to reset." [22]

The match against Polona was a wild ride. In the beginning, Coco struggled with how her opponent constantly changed the speed and spin of the ball. Sometimes the shots were coming at Coco hard and flat, but other times her opponent was using a slice shot that skidded off the grass and stayed low to the ground. Against Venus, there were a lot of longer rallies where they could both hit the ball hard from the baseline. This was a much different match, and Coco was struggling to get control of the points.

Not only did Coco lose the first set, but she fell behind early in the second as well. Down 5–2 and 30–40, Coco was one point away from going home. It still would have been a great tournament if it had ended right there. But something in Coco's mind told her she could still fight back.

After erasing the match point, Coco held serve but still needed to get a break right away to extend the match. She managed to do it—but barely, needing to fight off one more match point. Coco was living dangerously but managed to pull even at 6–6, which meant the set would be decided by a tiebreaker.

To win a tiebreaker, a player must win seven points before their opponent, but the tiebreaker isn't over unless they win by two. In other words, you can win a tiebreaker 7–5 or 17–15 but not 7–6. The reason for that is to ensure that the player who serves the first point doesn't have an unfair advantage. Even if you win all your serve points in the tiebreaker, you still have to win a point on return to win the set. The longest tiebreaker ever played in a professional tournament was 36–34, which is more points than a full set in most matches!

Thankfully, Coco didn't need a tiebreaker that long to pull even with Polona. At 8–7, Coco got the better of a thirty-two-shot rally and hit her chest with her fist as her parents celebrated in the players' box.

Still, the job wasn't done. Coco shot out to a 4–1 lead in the final set, but Polona pulled back even at 4–4. Coco held serve two more times to grab the lead back at 6–5. Finally, after playing for two hours and forty-six minutes, Coco got her first match point. After another long rally, Polona tried to draw her into the net with a short slice that barely cleared the top of the net. Coco sprinted forward to pick it off the ground. Polona responded with a lob over her head, and there was nothing Coco could do but watch. When ball sailed just past the baseline, Coco leapt into the air four times. The dramatic, back-and-forth battle only made the crowd love her even more.

When the numbers came in, 5.2 million people just in England had watched the match against Polona—by far the biggest audience of the tournament's first week. Coco was suddenly in the fourth round, and Cocomania was all the rage in England and around the world.

The day before her match against Venus, Coco had one fan ask to take a picture with her as she was leaving the practice courts. Now, everywhere she went at the All England Club, people were screaming her name and begging for autographs.

"It's pretty surreal how life changes in a matter of seconds," she said.[23]

Coco's Wimbledon run would last two more days. In the round of sixteen, she faced Simona Halep, the number-seven seed and a Grand Slam champion at the French Open one year earlier. This was a much bigger test than even Venus, and to nobody's surprise, Coco finally ran out of gas.

Though both sets were competitive, 6–3, 6–3, Simona was the better, more experienced player and had full control of the match from start to finish. In fact, just a few days later, she would go on to beat Serena in the final to claim her first Wimbledon title.

But for Coco, this run seemed like the beginning of something huge. The Centre Court crowd had fully embraced her, even sending her off with a standing ovation after the loss to Simona. Back home in America, she was the number-one topic on social media, even getting congratulatory Tweets from former first lady Michelle Obama.

"It's crazy how big this has gotten," Coco said.[24]

Suddenly, the conversation shifted to when fans would get to see Coco play again. Along with netting her more than $200,000 in prize money, making the fourth round at Wimbledon boosted her ranking from number 313 into the top 150—and every tournament in the world was going to want her to play.

Still, Coco was just fifteen. She had a great run in her first Wimbledon with no expectations on her. But now, she was going to be playing against the best women in the world on a regular basis. All of them were older and stronger than her, and now Coco was going to have a target on her back whenever she entered a tournament.

Living up to that standard with the world now watching her every move wasn't going to be easy.

"It's a huge thing that she's able to play in the fourth round of Wimbledon," Simona said. "I think if she keeps going, she will be top-ten soon."[25]

Coco was on her way, to be sure. But the journey to get there wasn't as smooth as anyone might have imagined that day.

CHAPTER 4

The skies in Paris were a perfect powder blue, with just a wisp of clouds hugging the top of the famous Eiffel Tower. It was a perfect day to celebrate Coco's high school graduation.

Unlike most kids who woke up every day and took the bus or carpooled to school, Coco's job playing tennis meant that she wouldn't be able to get a traditional education like a lot of her friends back in Delray Beach. Instead, thanks to Florida Virtual School's Flex program, she was able to take classes online and take her studies everywhere, no matter whether she was in Australia or the Middle East or Europe.

Even though Coco's schedule was determined by when she had to practice, travel and play matches, her mom and dad made sure that getting an education remained one of her top priorities. Even during tournaments, Coco used her down time to study and take exams.

"Both my parents graduated college, and my grandmothers are both teachers," she said. "I have a whole family really full of teachers. For college, I'm just going to think about that later on. But for now, finishing high school was important to me."[26]

Because tennis is such a difficult and competitive sport, with tens of thousands of kids around the world all trying to achieve the same dream, a lot of them give up on school at a pretty early age. All they want to think about twenty-four hours a day is tennis, tennis, and more tennis. Coco loved the sport as much as any of them, but she was raised to understand that sports don't last forever.

Candi, her mom, was a track star in high school. She got a scholarship to Florida State University and competed in the heptathlon, which combines the one-hundred-meter hurdles, the high jump, shot put, 200-meter dash, long jump, javelin throw, and 800-meter run. Her dad Corey played a lot of sports growing up, including some tennis. Later on, his focus turned to basketball, where he played on the team at Georgia State University and averaged 5.9 points per game.

Though both of Coco's parents reached a high level in sports, it wasn't a ticket to the Olympics or NBA stardom. What it did give them was a great education, setting them up for success in their careers—Candi as a teacher and Corey in the health care industry.

Coco was obviously going to be on a different path. At age eighteen, she had already won two tournaments on the WTA Tour, earned millions of dollars, and reached the top twenty of the world rankings. Still, it was important to both her and her parents to be a well-rounded young person and take her education seriously. Her dad, in particular, wanted her to learn about business.

"I know, like, on tour a lot of players don't always do that because you have tennis," Coco said. "Tennis is like what I do, but there's other interests that I have outside of tennis and definitely having knowledge on that can help me indulge in them more."[27]

With everything going on in her life, Coco was proud that she had done all the work necessary to complete high school. But because she was thousands of miles from home getting ready for a Grand Slam, she couldn't participate in a traditional ceremony where she could walk across a stage and get her diploma. Instead, she brought her cap and gown with her to Paris and took graduation pictures in front the Eiffel Tower, posting on Instagram: "I did it. No (cap emoji)."

In a way, it was fitting for Coco to celebrate such a big day in Paris, which she calls her favorite city in the world because of its history, its fashion, its unique architecture, and its delicious French food (she's particularly fond of croissants and foie gras).

But France was a special place in her tennis journey, too.

***

When she was ten years old, Coco flew all the way from Florida to the famous Mouratoglou Academy, a tennis paradise in the south part of France near the Mediterranean Sea. Players of all ages and from all over the world flock there because of its perfect weather, perfectly manicured courts, and the watchful eye of coach Patrick Mouratoglou.

Patrick has coached a lot of good players over the years, but his collaboration with Serena Williams made him one of the most prominent coaches in the world.

Serena found Patrick almost by chance. After losing in the first round of the French Open in 2012, Serena stayed in Paris to practice for a few days and reached out to Patrick to ask if she could use the facility he had built there.

At the time, Serena hadn't won a Grand Slam in two years and wasn't feeling very good about her game. Meeting Patrick changed everything. After a few days of talking and working together on the court, he became part of the team and traveled with her to Wimbledon a few weeks later. Serena won that tournament and the US Open as well. By the following year Patrick was officially her coach, helping her win ten Grand Slam titles.

Because he was always on television when Serena played tournaments, interest in Patrick's academy skyrocketed. Some of the best kids from all over the world even moved there, hoping Patrick and his staff of coaches could help them develop into pros. But training for a tennis career can be very, very expensive, and the Mouratoglou Academy cost more than the Gauff family could afford.

Because of how much success Patrick was having with Serena, he started a foundation to help pay for gifted young players who didn't have the resources to pay for full-time coaching. But getting one of those scholarships was highly competitive, and Patrick put all the kids through a variety of tests and practices to get a sense of their physical ability, how they played tennis and whether they could withstand the demanding lifestyle at the academy.

Maybe the most important part, though, was the one-on-one interview with Patrick. This is where Coco really shined.

"I want to feel their drive and belief in themselves," Patrick said. "She was looking at me in the eyes. I was asking tough questions because a lot of players say, 'I want to be number one,' but do they really believe it? And do they really understand what's behind it? To reach the top of the game is so difficult. There are a lot of ups and downs, and most of them don't really believe. I wanted to know that, and there she impressed me the most."[28]

Patrick believed Coco should start training at his academy and would pay for everything she needed. But he also believed it was important, especially at such a young age, to have a normal family life. The decision was made that Coco would train part-time in France to learn everything she could about tennis, practice with the best players of her age group and play some international junior tournaments. But for more than half the year, she'd go home to be with her parents and brothers. A coach from the academy would even go back to Florida with her so she could continue to progress when she was away from Patrick.

The coaching Coco received at the academy was different than what she got in America, where most of the training had focused on using her speed and power because that's the kind of game that works best for the asphalt or so-called "hard" courts that you can find at most country clubs and public parks.

In Europe, tennis players grow up learning the game on red clay, a softer surface made of bricks that have been crushed into a fine powder and spread all over the base of the court.

Because the clay is so slippery, it's important to learn different kind of movements like sliding into shots. Also, because the ball bounces higher off the clay, players naturally learn how use different spins and slices rather than the flat, powerful shots that skid through a hard court.

For a lot of American players, it can take years of experience to learn how to play on red clay. Because Coco had taken to it at such an early age thanks to Patrick's academy, it was almost second nature to her—another reason to love playing in France.

"For me, it's the movement," she said. "It's one of my strengths on other surfaces, but I think clay only enhances that. I really enjoy sliding. I think it helps me recover faster after I get to the ball."[29]

After a few years of going back and forth between Patrick's academy and Delray Beach, it was time for Coco to make her debut at the junior Grand Slams, which take place every year at the same place and the same time as the main Grand Slam tournament that everybody in the world watches on television.

Though the junior events aren't highly publicized, they are very important because it's where the power brokers in the tennis world go to identify up-and-coming talent. Tennis isn't just a sport; it's a business that uses a player's popularity to help sell the clothes they wear on the court or the kind of racket they use. All of those companies are looking for the next big thing, so they often sign the top junior players to sponsorship contracts in hopes that successful on the court as a pro will eventually help promote their brand.

Coco had experienced plenty of success in big junior tournaments, but the US Open junior championship proved that her future was bright. At just thirteen years old and playing mostly against girls who were sixteen or seventeen, Coco reached the final of the US Open without dropping a set. She lost 6–0, 6–2 to Amanda Anisimova for the championship, but not very many girls Coco's age had ever gone that far in such a big tournament. It was the kind of result that would force everybody in the sport to pay attention.

"I'll definitely be back here," she said.[30]

As much progress as Coco was making in the juniors, it was around this time that she began to doubt herself.

Maybe it was the pressure that was building up as she started to get more well-known around the tennis world. Maybe it was seeing all her friends post social media pictures of their normal junior high and high school experiences and realizing she would miss out on most of the things kids typically do like Friday night football games or going to the prom.

Maybe it was a little bit of burnout with a sport that had consumed most of her time since she was a little girl.

"I was struggling to figure out if this was really what I wanted," she wrote. "I always had the results, so that wasn't the issue, I just found myself not enjoying what I loved. I realized I needed to start playing for myself and not other people. For about a year, I was really depressed."[31]

A first-round loss in the Australian Open Juniors in January devastated Coco, and when she got home, she and her dad decided she would take a few months off of playing tournaments. Part of being successful in tennis is understanding that losing is part of the deal. Every week, only one player—the person who wins the tournament—leaves happy. Everyone else has to figure out how to let go of the disappointment and move on to the next match.

By the spring, Coco was ready to play again. And this time, when she entered the junior French Open, nobody could stop her.

Using all those clay court skills she learned at Patrick's academy, Coco beat some of the best juniors in the world to take the title. At fourteen years and two months of age, she was the fifth-youngest to ever win the tournament, putting her name alongside players like Martina Hingis, Jennifer Capriati and Gabriela Sabatini, all of whom won Grand Slams titles as professionals.

"I'm really happy and excited and also proud of myself for fighting," Coco said. [32]

Shortly after that, Coco signed a contract with New Balance to wear their shoes and clothing on the tennis court. Barilla, which sells pasta in almost every grocery store in America, also offered her a sponsorship deal. Even though Coco hadn't played in any big tournaments, companies expected her to become a star.

Just four years later, it looked like their investment was about to pay off in a big way.

***

The Eiffel Tower celebration of Coco's high school graduation brought back all the good Parisian vibes heading into the 2022 French Open. And as a bonus, she didn't have to worry about doing any more homework in between matches and practices!

By now, Coco had gotten used to playing at all the major tournaments, on all the big courts, and against all the top opponents. There had been a few disappointments after her big breakthrough at Wimbledon, and she still hadn't come close to winning a Grand Slam title. But at Roland Garros, the site of the French Open, she felt at home.

"I just like it here," she said. "I just like the clay here. I don't think there is any better clay in the world, in my opinion."[33]

Coco got through her first two opponents pretty easily, but usually the third round of Grand Slams is when the toughest matches start. This time, though, a lot of the highly ranked players were losing early on. By seeding, Coco would have expected to play former French Open champion Garbiñe Muguruza in the third round, number-five Anett Kontaveit in the fourth round, and the defending champion Barbora Krejčíková in the quarterfinals. Instead, all of them were knocked out before they could even face Coco.

Suddenly, Coco found herself in the quarterfinals playing Sloane Stephens, someone she had looked up to for a long time. They met in Florida when Coco was just getting serious about tennis, and Sloane—who was already on the pro tour at the time—took an interest in

Coco's development. She even came to Coco's tenth birth-day party, and their connection carried through all the way to the 2017 US Open. As Coco finished runner-up in the junior draw, Sloane shocked the world by winning the biggest title of her career.

Now they were on even footing, playing for a spot in the semifinals.

The first time they faced each other in a tournament, Sloane won easily. This time, Coco was determined to show that she could change tactics and learn from her past mistakes. Unlike their first match, Coco decided to take the initiative this time and play more aggressively to push Sloane backward behind the baseline. Then, when Coco had the opportunity, she'd change the rally either with a drop shot or by coming to the net for a volley to try and make Sloane uncomfortable.

It was a great plan, and it worked extremely well. After a close first set, Coco ran away with the match 7–5, 6–2 to make the semifinals of a Grand Slam for the first time. Afterward, she thanked Sloane for helping her understand what it would take to make her own way as a tennis player and not judge herself by what others expected.

"Even when I was young, it was the next Serena, next this, next that, and I think I really fell into the trap of believing that," she said. "It's important that you have high

hopes for yourself, but also at the same time, it's important to be in reality and I think that's where I am. I'm in
reality where I'm enjoying the moment and enjoying the
situation." [34]

A few days later, Coco would get another lesson in the
importance of living in reality. Though she had made the
final by easily beating Martina Trevisan, the last match of
the tournament would be by far the most difficult Coco
had ever played.

The opponent standing between Coco and the trophy
was Iga Świątek. Not only had Iga won the French Open
once before, she had taken over as the world's number one
player by winning thirty-four consecutive matches. On
clay especially, she almost seemed unbeatable.

Once the match began, Coco never had much of a
chance. After dreaming her whole life about what it would
be like to play a Grand Slam final, it was over in just six-
ty-eight minutes. Coco hadn't done anything wrong, but
Iga just overwhelmed her, 6–1, 6–3.

"She really didn't give me anything," Coco said. "Every
time I thought I hit a good ball, it wasn't."[35]

If Coco wanted to play in these types of matches and
win the biggest tournaments, she knew she had to get better. Only twenty-one years old herself, Iga was going to
be around a long time. If Coco wanted this to become a

rivalry, the only way was to raise her level. At that moment, she didn't feel particularly close.

In tennis, after every final at every tournament, the loser of the match is expected not only to give a speech, but to stick around long enough to watch the winner receive the trophy. Nobody enjoys that experience, especially at a Grand Slam when there's so much at stake.

For Coco, it was the first time experiencing that kind of disappointment, and it showed. She could barely get through thanking her parents and her team without starting to cry. But after the worst part was over and Coco stepped into the background, she turned her sights to the future.

As Iga accepted the silver cup given to the French Open winner and hoisted it over her head, Coco made sure to watch every second of the celebration and train her eyes on Iga's every move.

"I want to feel what that felt like for her," Coco would later reveal.[36]

The next time she had a chance to win a Grand Slam trophy, she wasn't going to let it go so easily.

CHAPTER 5

To play tennis at a high level, you need to master four basic strokes: the serve, the forehand, the backhand, and the volley. Though certain elements like good balance and footwork are always going to be necessary to execute a good shot, the interesting part of the sport is that no two people hit the ball or play the game exactly the same way.

Some players, like Roger Federer, hit a backhand with one hand on the racket. Monica Seles, one of the most talented women who ever played, had two hands on the racket for both her forehand and backhand. Most players are more comfortable rallying from the baseline, but the legendary John McEnroe was at his best when he could get to the net and use his quick reflexes to hit volleys. Nick Kyrgios popularized the underarm serve, which is supposed to barely dribble over the net and surprise players if they stand too far back to return.

Why does tennis have so much variety? While most players are taught basic techniques and habits from a young age, their games develop through years of repetition. Over time, they figure out what feels natural to them and learn how to use their strengths while minimizing weaknesses. There's no right or wrong way to play—as long as the ball goes in!

But as Coco Gauff started out on the WTA Tour and began to face some of the top players on a regular basis, opponents started to notice that they were more likely to get Coco to miss if they hit it to her forehand.

The forehand is the first shot any player learns because it's the one you hit with your dominant hand—the right hand for righties and the left hand for lefties. Because most people are stronger with their dominant hand, they can swing the racket more easily and use the speed of their arm and the whipping action of their wrist to put spin on the ball. That combination—the power of the racket and the spin created by the arm—is what allows the ball to pass over the net and then drop quickly into the court. Without the spin, which is created when the motion of the racket brushes upward, you'd be hitting a lot of balls into the fence.

For most top players, the forehand is the shot they hit with the most power and accuracy. In a match, they want to hit as many forehands as possible because it probably gives them the best chance to win.

Coco's game is just the opposite. Her two-handed backhand is smooth and compact, allowing her to direct it anywhere she wants. But when she hits the forehand, Coco sets up the backswing way behind her body and holds the grip so that the racket face is positioned the same way you'd find it laying on the ground.

Though this way of hitting a forehand helps generate more power and a high-bouncing ball that's difficult for an opponent to return, it requires perfect timing. If something is just a little bit off, or if a player is nervous and not hitting their forehand with a lot of speed, it can break down easily.

From the moment Coco started playing in pro tournaments, it was clear her overall game was good enough to win a lot of matches including her first WTA title at a small tournament in Austria in October of 2019. When tennis started up again after the COVID-19 pandemic in 2020, Coco entered the top fifty for the first time. The 2021 season started slowly, but she made enough quarter-finals and semifinals—with her second career tournament victory at an event in Italy—to end the year ranked number nineteen.

Though Coco was the youngest player in the top twenty by far, some critics started wondering whether she was progressing fast enough. After her big breakthrough at Wimbledon in 2019, Coco had played in eight more Grand Slam events. Only once had she reached the quarterfinals.

Coco knew that Serena had won her first Slam at age seventeen. Venus had done it at twenty. As 2022 began, with Coco about to turn eighteen and already having a lot of experience on tour, her goals were clear: it was time to win a Grand Slam.

"I definitely feel ready," she said.[37]

Right away, though, there was a disappointment. Coco's trip to Australia for the first Slam of the year ended after just one match when she lost to Chinese player Qiang Wang. Afterward, Coco admitted that she didn't play with the same freedom she had enjoyed previously and was thinking too much about what might happen if she missed. As a result, she made a lot of errors—especially with her forehand.

Players often don't want to focus too much about their weaknesses because they're afraid it will be in their head when they walk on the court. But because the rest of Coco's game was so good, every opponent knew that the best way to beat her was to make her hit as many forehands as possible. And the more they played that way, the more Coco had to think about her forehand. And the more she thought about it, the more tense she played and the more she missed.

It could be a vicious cycle.

Still, Coco showed up at every stop on the tour ready to grind, even on days where her forehand wasn't working so well. Though Coco didn't win a tournament in 2022, the season overall felt like another step in her progression with an overall record of thirty-eight wins and twenty-two losses. With the French Open final, the quarterfinals at the US Open, and a few other solid results, Coco did well enough to qualify for the WTA Finals, a prestigious event for the eight players who earned the most ranking points during the year.

"It means a lot to me," she said. "I busted onto the scene in a very big way, and a lot of people were having opinions on whether or not I would do well. I just think this proves all the work I've put in is paying off. It allows me to take a step back and realize I'm one of the top eight players in the world, and I should be grateful for that." [38]

***

The biggest thing that seemed to be holding Coco back from winning the big titles was her forehand. She could get away with it against the most of the weaker players. But heading into the 2023 season, her record against some of the top women wasn't too encouraging: 0–5 against number-one Iga Świątek, 1–4 against Maria Sakkari, 0–4 against Simona Halep, just to name a few.

If Coco wanted to win Slams, those were the types of players she needed to start beating.

Too often, though, Coco would get to a quarterfinal or semifinal and start missing her forehand. At the Madrid Open in the spring of 2023, Paula Badosa beat her 6–3, 6–0 in one of Coco's worst matches of the year. Afterward, Paula admitted that the top players all had the same gameplan against her: hit to the forehand as many times as possible.

"She plays amazing when she's defending," Paula said. "She's very fast. She has a crazy backhand, very good serve…But when you have like the [weak] spot there, you just go there. I just tried to go to her forehand, sometimes just give it to her and make her do more than what she can."[39]

It was obvious to everyone in tennis that it was becoming a real problem. The top players don't have many weaknesses at all, and this was clearly an area where Coco was struggling to get better. If anything, the situation was worsening tournament by tournament. For such an important stroke—studies show that around 75 percent of all shots hit in a match are either forehands or serves—Coco was going into a lot of these matches at a big disadvantage. Some commentators were even suggesting that she take six months off and learn a simpler technique and a less extreme grip that would perhaps be more reliable.

"Everybody talks about it," said Chris Evert, champion of eighteen Grand Slam titles and television commentator. "It's probably in her head by now."

It was obvious that Coco didn't enjoy all the conversation about her forehand, but every time she had a press conference at a tournament, it was one of the topics that was always going to come up.

Often, she would just change subject or spin it a different way.

"Obviously the forehand is something I need to improve on, but on clay especially I feel like it's one of my weapons," she said prior to the French Open. [40]

Heading into Wimbledon, Coco said the forehand was one of many things that should would continue working on.

"It's going to be a long process," she said. "It's tough to fix everything, you know, in between tournaments."[41]

The other problem was that Coco didn't have a full-time coach. Diego Moyano, who worked with her for a year, left the team in April. Patrick Mouratoglou agreed to help out a bit before the French Open, but he was already working with another player. At least for the time being, her dad was back in the main coaching seat.

But the results spoke for themselves. Coco wasn't just losing to the top players; she was starting to lose earlier in tournaments, even on clay where she felt the most comfortable.

Unlike the year before, when Coco arrived in Paris full of confidence and positive momentum, she was now in a slump and hoping to discover something that would turn her disappointing 2023 season around.

"I am a different person than I was last year," she said. "I think I just have to find the way I want to approach it for this version of myself now. That comes through trial and error. I feel like for some reason, though, I always seem to find that in Paris. I don't know if it's the city or the vibe here that makes me a lot more at ease."[42]

Though Coco played well at Roland Garros, she ran into Iga again in the quarterfinals. The match was pretty much the same as all of their other meetings, with Iga in control from start to finish. Coco admitted she was getting a little frustrated, not just with how she was playing but with her inability to do any damage when Iga was on the other side of the net.

"I have to figure something out," she said.[43]

Still, even that wasn't the low point of Coco's season.

When Coco arrived at Wimbledon and saw who she would be playing in the first round, she knew it was going to be tough. Sofia Kenin had been on the best players in the world a few years earlier, even winning the Australian Open right before the pandemic hit in 2020 and reaching a French Open final after that.

Kenin had been dealing with injuries for the past couple years but had started to get back in form and reached the Wimbledon main draw by winning three rounds of qualifying. Full of confidence on the grass, Sofia played some of her best tennis in years and took the first set, 6–4. Coco responded right away to win the second, 6–4. But in the third when it really got tense, Coco once again struggled to hit forehands cleanly. Even when they went in, they were dropping short in the court, allowing Sofia to take control of the points and push Coco from one sideline to the other. By the end, Sofia had been the much better player and was rewarded with a 6–2 victory in the decisive set. Coco was out of the tournament early once again.

"I feel like I have been working hard, but it's clearly not enough," she said. "I have to go back to the drawing board and see where I need to improve."[44]

***

Though Coco was out of the singles competition, she stayed in London for a few more days to play the doubles tournament. But something more important was happening behind the scenes to help Coco's game get back on track.

In tennis, most of the top players work with one or even two coaches on a full-time basis. The coaches are responsible for organizing practices, scouting opponents, and supporting their player from a seat near the court. They even give players tips and instructions about what they're doing right or wrong while the match is happening.

For a few months, Coco didn't have a coach other than her dad. A week before Wimbledon, though, the Gauff family brought a new coach named Pere Riba onto the team. They hoped he might be able to get Coco out of her slump in time for the next series of tournaments, which would all be played back in America. The biggest one, of course, was the US Open—the last Grand Slam of the year.

Though Pere was a former player who reached a high of number sixty-five in the world rankings, he did not have a long track record coaching top players like Coco. That wasn't the case with the next person the Gauff family wanted to add to the coaching team: Brad Gilbert.

In his younger days, Coach Brad wasn't the most gifted or most technically perfect player on the men's ATP Tour and would sometimes get frustrated about being unable to beat opponents who were more skilled or more athletic.

But at some point, Brad realized that tennis wasn't just a sport about who could hit the best forehands and backhands. He saw it as a battle of mental strength and tactics that could allow somebody like him to win matches against highly ranked players. If you could outthink your opponent, you could beat your opponent—even if they were better at hitting the ball.

Brad used his philosophy to have a great playing career, winning twenty tournaments on the ATP Tour and reaching a number-four world ranking at one point. Over time, other players hated to play against him because they knew it would be a totally different kind of match from what they were used to. Brad didn't always win, but he made opponents uncomfortable by finding their weakness and testing it time and time again.

Some would say that Brad Gilbert was even better as a coach than he was as a player. In the summer of 1994, he teamed up with Andre Agassi, who was one of the most famous players of his era but hadn't been living up to his potential. Just a few months after they started working together, Andre won the US Open.

Nine years later, the same thing happened: Andy Roddick hired Coach Brad and won the US Open almost immediately.

What better person to ask for advice?

Coach Brad had never met Coco before, other than a few short interactions around tournaments where he was a television commentator. So he was a bit surprised to a phone call one morning while working at Wimbledon from a sports agent representing Coco asking if he would be available to meet her and her parents before they went home to Florida.

Of course he'd be interested! Though he hadn't worked with any pro players in a few years, Coach Brad was open to getting back out on the tour if it was a good personality fit and the player had a chance to win big tournaments. He was convinced Coco was the kind of player he wanted to coach.

"She's a great kid," he said. "Probably her two most amazing qualities are she's incredibly humble and she's so dedicated, professional, and hardworking."

They all sat down and talked for about an hour. Coach Brad mentioned a few of the things he had noticed about Coco's game and areas where he might be able to help. He also said the rest of his summer was free after Wimbledon, and he'd be willing to try a partnership if Coco's team was interested.

A couple weeks went by and Coach Brad didn't hear anything more from the Gauffs. Then, as he was getting ready to leave his home in California to work at a tournament Washington, D.C., he got another phone call asking if he'd be willing to meet Coco somewhere for a two-day coaching audition.

As it turned out, Coco had entered the same tournament, so it would be a perfect opportunity to see if they could work together for the rest of the summer. Coach Brad had packed his suitcase planning to be gone for just a week. At the last minute, his wife told him he might want to bring his passport because the next tournament after Washington was in Canada. If things worked out with Coco, who knew the next time he'd be home.

When he arrived in Washington and got on the court with Coco, Coach Brad was immediately encouraged by what he saw. Over the years, he had seen so many struggling players lose their desire to work and practice because they weren't getting the results they wanted. With Coco, it was the exact opposite: she was hungry to train and willing to listen to everything he had to say.

"All she's thinking about is wanting to get better, and that's everything in tennis," he said. "It's not that I've got to win this tournament or that tournament. I think more than anything, she has a great attitude."

With three tournaments to play before the US Open and not much time to practice, Coach Brad knew he wouldn't be able to make any big changes in Coco's game. He had a few very small things in mind that she could easily bring with her onto the court, and he had ideas about new tactics that might help against certain opponents.

"The first thing I noticed is she's put in the work," he said. "Sometimes when you're struggling as a player that's one thing that can falter. We made a couple small tweaks in things."

Mostly, he wanted to get Coco in a better frame of mind after suffering some disappointing losses during the summer in Europe.

The one thing he wasn't going to do was worry too much about Coco's forehand.

CHAPTER

In Washington, D.C., after only a few days of working with Coco, her new coach Brad Gilbert had a vision.

"I think she's going to win the Open," he said.

He didn't tell many people, just one or two close friends. It wasn't like Coach Brad to make such big predictions, especially after he had just joined the team. But after the difficult summer Coco had experienced on the court, it was important to bring some positive vibes.

"If you don't think it, sometimes it can't happen," he said. "The talent was there. Just sometimes, little things can make a difference. She needed to get her mojo back."

But how? Coco had taken the loss at Wimbledon harder than anyone knew. Before the tournament, she felt like she was starting to play better tennis. She had high hopes of winning a few rounds and starting to feel like herself again. But after getting beat by Sofia Kenin, Coco began to question herself. Was she really as good as she thought? Did she have what it took to win a Grand Slam trophy and reach her dreams? Were the critics right that she wasn't getting any better as a player?

It didn't help that Coco, like a lot of people her age, was constantly on social media. After every loss, there would be a long list of insults that were hard to avoid but only made her feel worse.

"I just felt like people were, like, 'Oh, she's hit her peak and she's done. It was all hype,'" Coco said. "I see the comments. People don't think I see it, but I see it."[45]

The attacks were over-the-top, but some of the questions about Coco's future were fair. She wasn't a fifteen-year-old phenom anymore. Though a lot of nineteen-year-olds are just starting college and not even thinking about their careers yet, women's tennis is different. Coco had been competing against the best players in the world for quite some time, and while she had every reason to be proud of her accomplishments, it seemed like there was still a big gap between herself and the players at the very top of the rankings.

Though Coach Brad was already thinking about how Coco could win the US Open, she had much lower expectations for the rest of the year. When she got to Washington, Coco's mindset was to use the next few months to practice what her new coaches were teaching her and hopefully make some big improvements in 2024.

At first, the pairing of Coco and Coach Brad didn't make a lot of sense because they are such opposites. Most of the coaches Coco had worked with had been younger or closer to her parents' age, but he was sixty-two—basically old enough to be her grandfather—and hadn't worked with a top-level player out on the tour for ten years. Most of his success had come with players who were winning tournaments before Coco was even born. With such a big age gap, she was wondering if they'd be able to communicate with each other.

Coco had also picked up on all of Coach Brad's strange routines, and she found them quite amusing. For one thing, he didn't sleep very much—like, hardly at all. He would often be awake well before sunrise, full of energy and ready to go for an exercise walk. Whenever he referenced numbers, he was always very specific and exact: For instance, instead of saying, "It's almost 2 o'clock," he would say something like, "It's 1:57." Or if you asked him the odds of somebody winning a match, he'd never say sixty-forty, but maybe something like 61.23 percent. He didn't drink ice-cold water, only room temperature. And he constantly offered her Jolly Ranchers—a habit from his old playing days, where he would have one in his mouth during matches.

"I take them, but I don't eat them," she said. "I can't have Jolly Ranchers every five minutes!"[46]

Though they may have liked different shows or listened to different music, they were able to relate where it was most important: on the tennis court. And one thing Coach Brad noticed immediately was that Coco didn't smile very much when she was playing.

As serious as professional tennis can be, and as important as these tournaments are when you're playing for money and ranking points and big trophies, the reason people fall in love with the game when they're kids is because it's *fun*.

Sure, Coco was having a few problems with her game. It didn't feel good to lose matches she expected to win or to be sent home from Wimbledon after the first round. But Coach Brad made it clear that the biggest thing she could do for herself was to show the world and herself that she enjoyed being out on the court.

"When he said that, I was a little bit surprised," she said. "I started to think and I was like, 'Yeah, I do.' That's something I'm trying to work on."[47]

Coach Brad brought something else to the table that was different than most coaches. Tennis players are taught from a young age that they need to focus on their weaknesses and work as hard as they can to improve the things they're not good at.

With Coco, though, there were so many things that she could do well: she had one of the best backhands in the world, her serve could be a weapon if she was willing to hit it hard, and there was nobody on the women's tour who moved around the court any better or faster.

Everyone liked to talk about Coco's shaky forehand, but Coach Brad didn't see any reason to bring it up right away. He thought with the right game plan and a positive attitude, Coco could find ways to use her strengths more often and make her weaknesses seem less important.

More than anything, it seemed like a fresh start for Coco after a tough year. Wimbledon had been maybe the lowest point of her career, but with Coach Brad and Coach Pere Riba joining her team, there were reasons to feel the joy of playing tennis again. Plus, all the pressure was off now. Coco had no expectation of doing well in Washington or at any of the tournaments coming up. She knew she had a lot of work to do, but this was a new, exciting experiment. For the rest of the year, it didn't really matter if she won or lost.

***

Coco's phone wouldn't stop ringing. First, it was her brother Codey. She quickly answered his FaceTime request but hung up after a few seconds.

"Bro, I've got to call you later!" she said. Moments later, her father's number showed up on the caller ID.

"Oh my God!" she said.[48]

It wasn't a good time for Coco to talk. She happened to be in the middle of the winner's press conference right after the final of the Mubadala Citi D.C. Open.

Coming to Washington low on confidence and with little reason to believe she'd play well, Coco had done something spectacular and unexpected. She had won four matches—actually, she'd *dominated* four matches— to earn her fourth tournament title since becoming a pro on the WTA Tour. And it's not like Coco beat a bunch of nobodies. In the quarterfinals, she had to face Belinda Bencic, a Swiss player who had beaten Coco in their only previous meeting. Coco won easily, 6–1, 6–2. In the semifinals, she earned a 6–3, 6–3 win over another solid top-twenty player in Liudmila Samsonova. And in the final against Maria Sakkari, who had won four of their five matches before that, Coco played almost flawless tennis and took a 6–2, 6–3 victory. It was the best Coco had ever played from start to finish of a tournament.

In just a few days, the confidence she was lacking after Wimbledon had returned.

"I think it's pretty clear how everybody's going to play me on the scouting report," she said. "I have beaten that scouting report."[49]

She was, of course, talking about the forehand that had gotten so much attention earlier in the year. All of Coco's opponents in Washington tried to hit as many balls to her forehand as possible, hoping she would miss. But at this tournament, it wasn't happening like it did earlier in the year—and it was surprising to her opponents.

"Obviously, we all know that her forehand was always her weaker shot," Maria said. "I feel like now she's improving that. She's making more balls. She's solid. Mentally, she looks a lot more mature. She knows what she's doing on the court."[50]

Everyone wanted to know: what changed so quickly? Coco always had the talent, but she hadn't played like this consistently all year. And the truth was, she only had been on the court with Coach Brad for a few days. There wasn't enough time to make big adjustments to her game.

The secret wasn't much of a secret. In fact, Coach Brad had written an entire book about it called *Winning Ugly*. A lot of the book was about Coach Brad's own playing career and how he was able to beat all the top players of his era despite having a game that most experts would consider unusual. But the more important point he wanted to make was that tennis isn't a game about being perfect.

No matter if you're a pro, a college player, a junior trying to get better, or just someone who enjoys playing for fun, everyone experiences days when things don't work very well. Maybe your timing is off just a little bit or you don't feel great on the court, or you're struggling to hit one certain shot. In fact, there are probably more of those days in tennis than times where everything clicks. But you can't just give up and accept defeat. You have to figure out a way to compete when you're not at your best.

"Just live to see another day," Coach Brad likes to say.

What was important for Coco to understand is that anybody can win a tennis match when they're playing well. But what makes the great players different from everybody else is that they can win when they don't have their A game. That's why Grand Slams are so hard to win. It's very hard to have seven good days in a row. You have to have the right attitude and an understanding of how to play tactically when things aren't going your way.

More than anything else, that's what Coco was missing. She showed from the very beginning of her career—really from the first big match she played against Venus Williams at Wimbledon—that she could scrape and claw and fight when the pressure was on. But she was also very hard on herself when she didn't play well, and that tension built up in her game to the point where she couldn't beat other top players unless she was having a good day.

What could Coco rely on if her forehand wasn't working? Maybe in one match, she might need to hit harder serves and win some quick points with an ace or serves that her opponents couldn't return. Maybe in the next, she could try to hit more winners with her backhand. And no matter what, she could always rely on her speed around the court.

The message to Coco was simple: Play to your strengths, and don't take unnecessary risks trying to hit winners. If you have easy forehands with a lot of time to set up and rip the ball, go ahead. But if you're not sure, or it's a difficult shot, just try to get it back in play and keep the point going until you have a shot you feel comfortable with. If she could stick to that recipe, she wouldn't need to change much with her forehand for now because Coach Brad and Coach Pere kept telling her the rest of her game was good enough to win matches.

"Both of them really instilled a belief in my game," she said. "Bringing someone in, sometimes they feel like they need to change everything. But I think with both of them, it's not like big changes. They are really confident in my game so I think it makes me even more confident."[51]

Right away, it worked. And now Coco had a new trophy to take home—except, she wasn't actually going home. The next stop on the WTA Tour was in Montreal, Canada, and she was bringing something even more important with her than the silver sculpture they gave to the winner in Washington.

For the first time in a while, Coco believed in herself.

***

It's a good thing Coach Brad brought his passport because he wasn't headed home after a two-day trial. He was now on Team Coco for the rest of the summer, and there was more work to do to get ready for the US Open.

"I had a feeling in Washington she was going to have a great run," he said. "I was mentally prepared."

It's never easy to go from a tournament straight into to the next event. Especially when you win, there's not much time to celebrate or recover. Coco's final in Washington finished late on a Sunday afternoon, which gave her only Monday and Tuesday to travel and prepare for her first match in Canada. But it was a good problem to have— much better than losing in the first round and having to wait a long time to play again.

The quick turnaround didn't seem to bother Coco too much. She picked up right where she left off in Washington, beating Katie Boulter 6–2, 6–2. Coco was just as impressive the next day against newly crowned Wimbledon champ Markéta Vondroušová, winning 6–3, 6–0 even though the match was delayed by seven hours because of rain. But her hot streak finally ended in the quarterfinals against Jessica Pegula, her good friend and doubles partner.

Coco wasn't too disappointed in her performance because it was a close match that came down to a handful of points in the third set. Plus, she was happy for Jessica, who went on to win the tournament. Because of how much time they spend together practicing and traveling to the same tournaments, it was important that they show respect, display good sportsmanship and be happy for each other when they played in singles.

"You fight your hardest on the court, and off the court everything is cool," Coco said. [52]

With Canada behind her, it was time to head for Cincinnati, which is always the last big tournament before the US Open. For Coco, it was another test to see whether she could keep the momentum going against a tournament field with all the best players in the world. And after three pretty easy victories, Coco was going to get the biggest test of all: another matchup with Iga Świątek.

This time, though, it wasn't the same Coco. She had learned to embrace the highs and lows, the praise, and even the haters. She no longer felt like she had to compare herself to Serena Williams or anyone else. She was starting to appreciate every step in the process, even the losses, because they were all a part of getting to whatever destination was intended for her.

"The worst thing that can happen is I lose," she said. "I try not to put too much on it. Obviously, you get nervous, but at the end of the day, I try to just think about making the moment as small as possible."[53]

It wasn't small to the rest of the world. Coco's 7–6, 3–6, 6–4 win over Iga was one of the most important results of the year in tennis, and not just because it was her first win in the rivalry after eight losses. With Coco's new coaches helping her become more confident and understand how she needed to play, she was getting better with every match.

And she was also growing up. As Coco played the final of Cincinnati against Karolina Muchová, a Czech tennis player, it was noticeable that her parents were not seated in the players' box like they had been in nearly all of the big matches she ever played. For most of Coco's tennis career, her mom and dad were the biggest parts of her team. They had started her in tennis. They had sacrificed their own careers and lives to set Coco up for success. And they had been behind her all the way as she rose to the top ten in the world.

But now, it was time to take a step back and let Coco be an independent young woman on the world stage, with a professional team of coaches now entrusted to help her go even further.

After Coco won the title in Cincinnati, the biggest of her career so far, she accepted the trophy and made sure to mention the two most important people in her life, who wouldn't be there to celebrate the moment.

"My mom—I love you so much for being my emotional support," she said. "She's not here. And my dad, he's also not here, but he is the reason why I am here today. He is the reason why I play tennis. He is the reason why I believe I can do this."

Now, everybody believed she could do it. After a few years of wondering when Coco would reach the top of the sport, it suddenly felt close. With two tournament trophies and wins over some of the best players in the world, this was now the Summer of Coco.

Seven matches stood between her and a Grand Slam title, and winning them wasn't going to be easy. But in just a few short weeks, Coco's season had gone from a disappointment to something exciting for the entire sport.

Now, it was time to go to New York.

CHAPTER 7

With the noise and commotion and the huge throngs of people everywhere you look, the US Open is intimidating enough on a normal day. The hours before Coco's first match, though, were anything but normal. As she got ready to play Laura Siegemund, Coco noticed that a security team was looking all over Arthur Ashe Stadium. And they weren't just any security guards, but the kind that wear dark jackets and sunglasses. That meant somebody very, very important was going to be there to watch her play.

Through the entire match, Coco didn't notice who it was in the crowd because she was so focused on the task at hand. But as soon as it was over and Coco left the court, somebody with the U.S. Tennis Association pulled her aside and let her know that somebody wanted to say hi: former first lady Michelle Obama, who was there to take part in the ceremony honoring Billie Jean King and the fiftieth anniversary of equal pay for men and women at the US Open.

The first lady had always been a big supporter of Coco, posting about her several times on social media. But Coco was shocked when she walked in the little room off the side of the court and saw former president Barack Obama as well.

"I think I'm going to never forget that moment for the rest of my life," she said.

Meeting the former president and first lady put Coco in a much better mood than she was in walking off the court. Even though she won the match, it took three sets—3–6, 6–2, 6–4—and had been a pretty frustrating experience from start to finish.

"I definitely won ugly tonight," she said.[54]

Coco didn't think she had played very well, but it was more than that. Laura, her opponent, had gotten under Coco's skin with a few tactics that almost seemed like they came out of the Coach Brad playbook. She played a lot of unusual shots like slices that stayed low to the ground and took Coco out of her rhythm. She rushed the net looking to pick off volleys, which not many players do these days, especially in the women's game. And she took as much time as possible between points, slowing the match down to a crawl.

In tennis, one of the most important rules is that the server controls how much time is taken between points. At the US Open and other pro tournaments, it's somewhat controlled by a clock. After a point ends and the umpire announces the score, a clock on the scoreboard starts counting down from twenty-five to zero.

The server can take all twenty-five seconds if they want, but if they haven't started their service motion by the end of the timer, they are supposed to receive a warning. If they do it a second time, they lose a first serve as a penalty.

The important thing is, no matter whether a player is going quickly or taking their time between points, the returner is supposed to be ready when the server is ready. But there's a catch: the server isn't supposed to hit the ball until the other player has established a return position and they've made eye contact. It's good sportsmanship to make sure everybody's ready to play, but it's also up to the umpire to make sure everyone is playing by the rules and one player isn't slowing the other one down too much.

But throughout the match, Coco and her coaches felt like Laura was taking advantage of the officiating—not just taking too long on serve but also trying to disrupt Coco's pace when it was her turn to serve.

"I felt like the rules were being bent," Coco said.[55]

It was all part of Laura's game plan. She was the underdog, ranked number 121 in the world, and to have a chance to win, she needed to make Coco feel uncomfortable. After the first set, it was obvious she was succeeding. After all the hype around Coco after Cincinnati, she was just one set from going home and having to face another big disappointment at a Grand Slam.

But that also meant it was time to focus on her own game and not worry about the rules. Any player knows that it rarely works out well when you're thinking about something other than hitting the ball. If you start to worry about missing, that's when you usually miss more. Coco couldn't let herself fall into the trap. She just needed to relax.

"I didn't think she was playing that poorly," Coach Brad said. "A point here or there and she could have won the set."

The cruelty of tennis is that entire matches can be decided by who wins a couple of key points. But the beauty of it the sport is that matches can change by the same small margins. That's why players who are losing should never give up. You just don't know when the door might crack open just enough to start a comeback.

***

That moment for Coco was obvious at the start of the second set. For nearly twenty-six minutes, she and Laura went back and forth, and back and forth, and back and forth a few more times—neither one able to take just this one game. Every time Coco had a break point, Laura would do just enough to fight it off. When Laura had chances to win the game and hold serve, she either made a mistake or Coco came up with a winner. They went to deuce twelve times until, finally, Laura made two mistakes in a row and lost the game.

After watching such a battle—thirty points in total!— the fans rose to their feet and gave Coco a standing ovation. It was just what she needed. Even though it was only one game and Coco was still losing on the scoreboard, she had regained the mental advantage.

But as Coco started to figure things out and take control of the match, Laura's pace of play got slower and slower, in part because the long game had made her tired. On serve, she was taking all twenty-five seconds between points. When she was returning, Coco would be standing up at the line ready to start the point while Laura was still walking around at the back of the court or off to the side where they keep the towels. On a hot, sticky summer night like this one, the chair umpire will sometimes allow a few extra seconds so that players have a chance to wipe the sweat off their faces and hands.

Everyone in the stadium, though, knew that Laura was stretching the rules to the absolute limit. It was yet another attempt to get Coco frustrated and hope she'd lose her concentration. Even Coach Brad and Coach Pere were urging Coco to say something to the umpire, which she really didn't want to do because she had won the second set and was up 3–0 in the third. If she could just ignore Laura's antics a little longer, maybe she could just win the match quickly and get back in the locker room without any problems. Complaining to the officials isn't really in her nature, anyway.

"I didn't want to break the momentum," she said. [56]

But finally, Coco couldn't take it anymore. After losing the point at 40–30, Coco was ready to serve at her normal speed, and as usual, was waiting as Laura walked away with her back turned to the court, her fingers adjusting the strings on her racket. When she finally turned around, Coco immediately went into her service motion and hit the ball. Laura put her hands up in the air and looked at the umpire, saying she wasn't ready. The umpire agreed with Laura and said Coco had to redo the serve.

The fans began booing and whistling at the call. They were just as impatient with Laura's slowdown tactics as Coco was. Suddenly, we had controversy in the stadium. It was time for Coco to stand up for herself.

"She's never ready when I'm serving; she went over to talk [to her coaches] like four times. You gave her a time violation once. How is this fair?" Coco said as she approached the chair umpire.

"It's not like we're playing long points! You're calling the score like six seconds after the point is over!"

Just like that, the booing in the crowd turned to cheers. The fans were itching to see Coco argue, and now here she was laying her cards on the table.

"She's never ready!" Coco continued. "It's not like we're having thirty-ball rallies!"

"You're very quick, she's very slow," the umpire tried to explain. Coco wasn't having it.

"No, I'm going a normal speed! Ask any ref here. I go a medium-paced speed!"

The umpire tried to respond, but Coco quickly cut her off, saying everyone in the stadium could see what was going on.

"I've been quiet for whole match! Now it's ridiculous. I don't care what she's doing on her serve! But my serve she has to be ready!"

Coco had made her point respectfully and forcefully, but it wasn't the end of the drama. Even though Coco seemed to have things under control, the agitation was written all over her face because the match was still crawling along at Laura's pace.

Finally, though, the pressure she put on the umpire finally paid off. At 4–1, 40–0, Coco was ready to serve when Laura once again turned around and went to the back of the court. Coco tapped her toe and pursed her lips, making sure everybody in the crowd knew she was unhappy that she had to wait one more time. The booing started up again. Then the umpire's voice came over the microphone.

"Time violation. Point penalty, Ms. Siegemund."

By awarding the point and thus the game to Coco, the score was now 5–1. Laura had a quizzical look on her face and began to walk toward the umpire. Now it was her turn to argue that she wasn't playing too slow but instead, it was Coco's fault for playing too fast!

At this point everyone was mad, and Coco looked distracted by everything that was going on. Though she was still just a game away from winning, her 5–1 cushion had suddenly become 5–4. Coco no longer had any room for error. If she didn't hold serve in the next game, it was going to be tied and Laura was going to believe she could actually win.

Coco got lucky on the first point. Laura had drawn her into the net with plenty of room to hit a passing shot crosscourt, but she smashed it well long of the baseline for 15–0. Coach Brad, who was beginning to get nervous and fidgety in his seat, flashed a slightly relieved smile and closed his eyes as if he was praying just to get this match over with.

On the next point, Coco got a short ball and rushed the net again. This time, she stretched out beautifully to her right to pick off Laura's passing shot and dipped it softly over the net for a 30–0 lead. Coco let out a deep breath and clenched her left fist.

The feeling of relief didn't last long. Suddenly, it was 30–all. The next point might be the most important of the match. The crowd clapped nervously. Coach Brad closed his eyes again. Coco needed a great serve. She got it! The radar gun clocked it at 114 miles per hour—one of her hardest of the match!—and Laura couldn't get the ball in play. Finally, after almost three hours on the court, it was match point.

***

When Laura's final backhand went into the net and Coco realized she had won, she felt all the tension that had bottled up over such a strange night rush out of her body all at once. But she also felt a sense of justice because she didn't let Laura or the umpire take advantage of her. Before coming to talk to the media, Coco watched a replay of the incident on her phone as she sat in the recovery ice bath. She was more convinced than ever that she was right to speak up but admitted that maybe she should have done it a bit earlier. What she had debated in the moment was whether saying something might make people look at her as a bad sport for complaining. Coco cared a lot about being a good role model and showing courtesy toward her opponents and the officials.

"It's stuff I think about, honestly. I know if you do one wrong move, people are going to call you all types of names and tear you down," she said. "Today I think it was important to show you can do all this, still stick to your ground, and people are going to respect you. I think as long as you approach a person with respect, then everything should be fine." [57]

Laura came in to talk to the media after Coco and had a much different perspective. At thirty-five years old, she had been on the tennis tour for a long time and played many countries and in all kinds of stadiums. She felt like the crowd's treatment of her had crossed over from being pro-Coco to disrespectful with the amount of booing and jeering she received for being a slow player. They even sometimes clapped when Laura missed a first serve, which annoys almost all tennis players because it's considered bad manners.

"I was very disappointed," she said. "I thought I'd go out there and have a great time on Ashe. I have to say I have not a good time, and that was just [because of] the audience."[58]

Laura had never been very emotional in front of the media before, but the more she talked about what she felt was unfair treatment, she couldn't stop herself wiping away some tears. Even though she lost, she was proud of herself for the tennis she played and the effort she put into trying to beat a younger and better player and the fight she had shown all the way to the last point. She wanted the fans to acknowledge that kind of effort and the great show that both players had given them. Instead, she was treated like a villain because they were rooting for Coco to win.

"As a tennis player, you are a performer. You owe the people, you owe the kids that watch, you owe the people that buy tickets for a lot of money," she said. [59]

Now, Laura was sobbing.

"At the end of the day, I go home and I can look at myself and say I did a great job," she said. "But did I get anything from the people for that? Right now, it feels pretty much like a flat zero because they treated me bad. They treated me like I was a cheater, like I was trying sneaky ways to win this match. They treated me like I was a bad person."[60]

Coco didn't want the crowd to be disrespectful to Laura either, but she did learn another valuable lesson about overcoming strange circumstances. From the very beginning with the security guards and wondering which VIP was going to be in the crowd that night to losing the first set to the out-of-character confrontation with the umpire, Coco was just glad to get through the first round.

For Coach Brad, it brought back some memories. When he won the US Open coaching Andre Agassi twenty-four years earlier, it was all about fighting back. In one match after the other, Andre found himself in difficult spots, even against players he probably should have beaten easily. But in the Grand Slams, especially when you're one of the favorites, you're getting everybody's best shot.

What matters isn't whether you fell behind early, it's whether you had the ability to find solutions.

"Sometimes out of nowhere, these matches get complicated and you have to find a way," he said. "I just think more than anything winning is contagious and when you're winning you find ways to win and when you're struggling and not winning that much, you find ways to lose."

On a night she didn't have her best stuff and there were distractions all around her, Coco found a way to win. Her resilience was a great sign moving forward into the rest of the tournament, but it was still only one match. If Coco wanted to make it all the way to the final, she was going to have to raise her level of play even higher.

"I think most of the time, every Grand Slam, you have one bad match," she said. I'm glad I was able to get that out of the way in the first round."[61]

In some ways, though, the challenges were just beginning.

CHAPTER

Moments before players emerge from the tunnel into the vastness of Arthur Ashe Stadium, they see a plaque with some of the most famous words in sports: "Pressure is a privilege."

It was a phrase made famous by Billie Jean King, and she said it often whenever someone asked her about spending most of her life in the spotlight as a tennis player and an advocate for equal rights. Yes, the pressure on athletes to win and perform and live in the public eye can be immense. But having that pressure means you are good at what you do and a lot of people believe in you. The pressure simply comes with the opportunities you get as an athlete, so why not embrace it?

Billie Jean knew what she was talking about. She won twelve Grand Slam singles titles, another sixteen in women's doubles, and eleven in mixed doubles. She also won a match under more pressure than probably any women's player ever on September 20, 1973, when she played Bobby Riggs in a match called the "Battle of the Sexes."

As Billie Jean fought for women to be paid as much as the men, Bobby Riggs mocked her and wanted to set up a match hoping to prove that even a fifty-five-year-old man who was retired from pro tennis could beat the best women's player in the world. Billie Jean finally agreed to the offer, and they played in front of thirty thousand people with fifty million more watching on television in the United States alone.

If Billie Jean lost, she was afraid that all the hard work she had done to start the WTA tour and have women's tennis taken seriously would go down the drain. She had never felt more pressure in her entire life.

In some ways, the tennis career Coco was privileged to have became a possibility for her and thousands of other girls because Billie Jean won the Battle of the Sexes. These days, the best women's basketball players can earn a living in the WNBA. The best women's soccer players have the National Women's Soccer League and the Women's World Cup. There is a worldwide tour for women's golfers. Other sports like volleyball and softball are growing every year.

But because of what Billie Jean accomplished, tennis had a head start on all of them and became the best opportunity for women to earn a living as an athlete and play in front of thousands of people all over the world. It also meant that for players in Coco's generation, the pressure wasn't about being able to make enough money to support their career or gaining the respect of men like Bobby Riggs. It was a different kind of pressure, but it was still very real.

For Coco, the second round of the US Open came with a type of pressure she had not experienced very much in her career. All the way from the time she burst onto the scene, she had been the young up-and-coming star trying to unseat the more experienced player.

But against Mirra Andreeva, the roles were reversed. Coco was the nineteen-year-old veteran, and Mirra was the charming sixteen-year-old with nothing to lose.

"I never thought about it before when I was on the younger end, and I never thought about in the past when I was on the older end," Coco said. "It means nothing."[62]

Still, if anyone knew what it was like to be in Mirra's shoes, it was Coco. In fact, nobody so young had made such a big impact in women's tennis since Coco's fourth-round run at Wimbledon in 2019 that turned her into a worldwide star.

Just like Coco, Mirra was a natural in the spotlight. Even though she was born and raised in Russia, she spoke almost perfect English, loved being interviewed by the media, and always had funny things to say. But she also had a lot of game, which she proved by making the third round at the French Open and the fourth round at Wimbledon in her first two Grand Slams.

Forget the age difference—this could be a dangerous match for Coco if she didn't take it seriously.

"At nineteen, you're not used to playing someone three years younger," Coach Brad said. "But you can't treat her as a sixteen-year-old. This is someone who is going to be top ten, top five in the future. So you have to treat the match like it's a tough opponent."

The good news for Coco is that they'd already played once before, with Coco winning in three sets at the French Open. She knew exactly what kind of challenge it would be.

Even though the final score of 6–3, 6–2 made it look like an easy win for Coco, the match was a little more interesting than that. Mirra broke Coco's serve in the very first game and was a point away from winning a couple more games in the first set that might have made the match complicated. But in all the important moments, Coco was the more solid player and didn't make many mistakes. The age and experience worked in her favor, but she had no doubt Mirra was an opponent that would be capable of beating her in the future. Coco already had rivals like Iga and Aryna, and it wouldn't be long until Mirra joined that group.

"I really see myself in her," Coco said. "Playing a younger person just reminded me how far I have come and I should be proud of myself. That process is necessary, and those losses are necessary for growth."[63]

Part of that growth, of course, was learning how to embrace a different kind of pressure than she had ever felt before. Through two matches, Coco was right on schedule.

***

The third round of a Grand Slam is when things start to get really interesting. Sometimes there are a lot of upsets in the first two rounds, paving the way for lower-ranked players to have a life-changing moment. But if the favorites win, the third round is when the higher-ranked players start to face each other.

Coco's third-round opponent was Elise Mertens, someone she had beaten both times they played in prior tournaments. Even though Elise was ranked right around the top thirty, Coach Brad was happy with the matchup.

"I would never have said it out loud," he revealed later, "but I felt like it was going to be one of those matches like I had seen in Washington or Cincinnati where Coco won easy."

Just like in the first round, Coco got placed on Arthur Ashe Stadium to open up the night session in front of a rowdy crowd that also expected her to dominate. But once again after the first set, Coco found herself walking a tightrope between victory and defeat.

Part of what had changed for Coco leading up to the US Open was that opponents were starting to do things against her that they'd never tried before. In a way, it was a sign of respect for how well Coco had done in Washington and Cincinnati. Just like Laura Siegemund, Elise came onto the court hoping to surprise her with a little different style of tennis than what Coco had expected.

Typically, Elise is more of a defensive player. She'll let her opponent dictate the rallies and move all over the court and wait for opportunities to end points. That's how Elise plays in pretty much every match, and that's what Coco was prepared for. But this time, Elise came out with the mindset to be more aggressive, which meant hitting closer to the lines and taking more risk. For thirty-nine minutes, it worked. Elise won the first set, 6–3, and yelled "Let's go!" at the top of her lungs when Coco's shot sailed long on set point. She was fired up, and everyone on Team Coco was stunned.

"She was playing much bigger and more aggressive-minded than I had scouted her," Coach Brad said. "She was taking it to Coco. It wasn't like Coco was losing as much as Mertens was playing a tremendous match."

Could she keep it up? That's always the question when a lower-ranked player is beating a higher-ranked player. Someone as good as Elise is fully capable of winning a set off all the best players in the world. But winning two sets is a different story. Coco had to raise her level of play with a little more accuracy and a little more power just to see if Elise could keep her hot streak going.

Things didn't much better at the start of the second set. After Elise held serve, Coco faced a break point and had a look on her face like she wasn't sure exactly what to do other than wait for her opponent to cool off. Then again, if Coco lost this game, she might just run out of time and be out of the US Open.

"Be aggressive when you have to be aggressive and change the rhythm when you have to change the rhythm," Coach Pere yelled from the stands. "Come on! Be positive! That's going to do it! Let's go!"

Finally, Elise made a mistake. On break point, Elise missed a forehand she would probably make ninety-eight times out of one hundred. It wasn't a complicated shot, and it was from right in the middle of the court. But after being so aggressive the entire match, she finally played a little bit safe and didn't accelerate her racket through the ball—a sign of either nerves or getting a little bit tired. For the first time all night, Coco saw what she needed to do.

Even if she missed a couple, it was time for Coco to start ripping the ball with her backhand and see if Elise could react quickly enough to handle such a big, heavy shot. When Coco finally held serve after saving five break points, mixing in some great backhand winners with powerful first serves, her entire mood changed from being frustrated to having a clear idea of what it was going to take to pull another match out of the fire.

The problem was, Elise just wouldn't go away. Every time Coco pulled ahead, Elise came right back. This second set was going to be tense right until the end, but it's exactly what Coco signed up for. Pressure is a privilege, right?

By the end of the second set, Coco had done exactly what great champions do. She hadn't gotten impatient or let herself be consumed by negative thoughts just because her opponent was playing better than her normal level.

Instead, Coco stayed patient, fought hard, and made the match as long and as physically demanding as possible until Elise finally ran out of energy.

From 4–3 in the second set, when Coco had to fight off more break points to stay in the lead, she didn't lose another game. By the end of the third set, which Coco won 6–0, Elise was so tired she could barely win a point.

The slow starts were becoming the theme of Coco's US Open. But so was her toughness when she got in trouble and in the moments where the match could go in either direction. Of course, she was hoping for some easy wins along the way. On the other hand, coming through these close matches was giving her a world of confidence that she could handle anything this tournament might throw at her.

"I'm figuring out these situations, making it easier and easier as the matches go," she said. "I think she played some of her best tennis she's played this season in the first two sets. When I'm not playing my best but still able to figure out how to win these matches, it's good."[64]

***

Just sixteen players were left in the tournament, and Coco was one of them. But so was Iga and Aryna and Jessica Pegula and Ons Jabuer, each of whom could win the title. Coco had faced all of them many times before, so she knew what she was up against. But the player she was about to face was a bit of a mystery.

Coco, of course, had watched Caroline Wozniacki many times before. After all, Caroline had been number one in the world once before and won the Australian Open in 2018. But a couple years after that, she announced that she was leaving tennis. Caroline had been struggling with injuries and was ready to have a family with her husband, former NBA player David Lee. Just like Serena, Coco never got a chance to play her.

But a few months before the US Open, Caroline announced that she was coming out of retirement and believed she still had the ability to win big tournaments. Caroline's return was big news. She was one of the most popular players in the world during her career and had been extremely successful for many years, even though it took her a long time to finally win a Grand Slam title.

What kind of player would she be now after sitting out for more than three years and having two children? Well, she was good enough to win three matches, including an upset over number-eleven seed Petra Kvitová in the second round. Caroline's return was becoming a pretty big story because it takes a lot of time and effort to get back on the court after becoming a mom. Plus, she was playing some pretty good tennis—surprisingly good given the circumstances.

"I guess I always had the belief in myself," she said. "It takes a little time just to get back into the match rhythm. Would I have been surprised had I lost in the first round? No. Would I be surprised if I keep winning? Also no. If I play my best tennis, I know I'm tough to beat. Someone has to play really well."[65]

Growing up watching Caroline play, Coco knew exactly what that meant. Caroline is the type of player that gives you nothing on the court. Though Caroline doesn't necessarily have the big forehand or serve that wins points quickly, she is one of the fittest and fastest players ever in women's tennis. Her consistency and ability to play for hours without getting tired always makes her difficult to beat. And that was exactly the point: Coco had to beat her because Caroline was never going to beat herself.

"Playing a legend like her is really exciting," Coco said. "I'm not going to take the moment for granted."[66]

This time, even without a slow start, Coco nonetheless found trouble. After winning the first set 6–3, she knew that Caroline was not going to panic. If anything, Caroline was getting even more patient, content to keep the ball mostly in the middle of the court and see if she could bait Coco into making some errors at the end of long points.

Coco felt like she had put in the training to run and play tennis for however many hours it took, but Caroline was right with her in that department. What made Caroline different was her mental discipline. When you play one long point after another and can't get the ball past her, the game can get boring. There's a natural impulse to start trying to hit more winners, which played right into Caroline's hands for years and years when she was at the top of the game.

"She banks on your mistakes," Coco said. "I was trying to tell myself just to be ready to play an extra ball because she's a player that even when you think you win the point, it's not over."[67]

Little by little, Coco's mistakes were piling up—especially with her old nemesis, the forehand. When Caroline won the final three games of the second set to even the match, Coco was once again in the middle of a battle that could go either direction. The good news was that she had been there before. The bad news was she didn't agree with what Coach Brad was directing her to do.

"Please, just stop," she told him as the second set slipped away.

Their disagreement continued in the third set after Caroline broke serve to take a 1–0 lead, putting Coco in some trouble. Coach Brad kept insisting that she play

Caroline's style of game: put more air under the ball, keep it in play, try to win longer points. On court, though, Coco felt that wasn't going to be a path to victory.

"I definitely agree that playing longer points is to my advantage," she said later. "But I felt in that moment, playing Caroline, watching her play so many years, that's what she feeds off of." [68]

As much as Coco trusted Coach Brad's knowledge of the game, and as much success as they had in a short amount of time, this was her match to win or lose. She was going to have to live with the result, and she was going to do it playing the way she felt gave her the best chance on this particular day. She was going to go for her shots and start taking some risks to try and win points. If it wasn't good enough, so be it.

"There was a little lump in my throat," Coach Brad admitted. "But the last six games of that set, Coco probably played her best tennis of the whole tournament. And she needed to because Caroline was that good."

From the moment she started ignoring his advice until the end of the match, it was all Coco blazing a trail of winners all over the court. Yes, it was risky. But in the end, it was a 6–3, 3–6, 6–1 win to be proud of not just because of the opponent, but because she trusted her instincts to change the game plan, took the responsibility on her own shoulders, and executed the shots when it mattered.

"People consider me sometimes someone who plays more passive," Coco said. "But I definitely think this tournament I've been winning the matches off of being the aggressor. Today it showed I can play aggressive, and I know that's probably when I play my best tennis. I was finding that balance."[69]

It hadn't been easy, but for four straight matches, Coco had risen to the occasion just like Billie Jean whenever there was a new challenge in front of her. Pressure was a privilege Coco had learned to enjoy, and it was only going up from here.

CHAPTER 9

The match everyone anticipated when the US Open draw came out looked for sure like it was going to happen. Coco had beaten Caroline Wozniacki to reach the quarterfinal, and now number one, Iga Świątek, was just one win away from getting the rematch she wanted. But did Coco want it? Coco had proven in Cincinnati she could beat Iga. On the other hand, it's not very often Iga loses twice in a row to the same player, and Coco's record against her was still just 1–8.

Either way, it was out of Coco's hands. If she wanted to win the tournament, she was going to have to beat the best players at some point. It would have been crazy to expect anything else.

But sometimes, crazy things happen—especially against Jeļena Ostapenko.

Everyone in tennis, even the best player in the world, has an opponent that just drives them up the wall. For Iga, that opponent is Jeļena. But what is it about Jeļena that makes Iga so uncomfortable? It's probably because they are so opposite in the way they go about things.

Iga likes things to be very structured on the tennis court. She thinks about the game very deeply and knows exactly the right shot to hit at the right time. When she's not playing, she works hard on the mental side of tennis to keep her emotions under control and travels to every tournament with a sports psychologist. There is nothing about Iga's game or her training that hasn't been debated and calculated to the greatest degree.

Jeļena, by contrast, is all about creating chaos—with her game and her personality. She plays completely fearless and sometimes random tennis, swinging as hard as she can at nearly every ball. It doesn't seem like she has much of a plan other than trying to hit winners all the time. When she's on, there's almost nothing you can do against her. But if she's even a little bit off, she can get knocked out by players nobody ever heard of before. You never know which Jeļena you're going to get.

Jeļena is also known for being loud: with the grunting sound she makes when she hits the ball, with the squeaky shuffling of her feet before she leaned into a return, with her neon-yellow clothing and with her complaints about the electronic line-calling system used at the US Open. Even when the cameras said that Jeļena hit a ball out, she often rolled her eyes and disagreed.

Jeļena's unpredictability ruffled the prim-and-proper Iga during the three matches they had played before. Though Jeļena had won all of them, surely Iga was ready this time. After a 6–3 first set, the rematch with Coco seemed like it was on. But then, almost out of nowhere, Jeļena went Jeļena and the winners started flying off her racket. Her big swings were landing in the court, making Iga play the kind of rushed tennis she hates, and Jeļena found sharp-angled shots that skidded low off the court and were impossible for Iga to chase down.

Then, almost without explanation, Iga's game just fell apart. Usually, even if things were going wrong in a match, Iga would try to change something or find a solution. That's how you get to number one in the world. But in this match, things were going quickly from bad to worse. Jeļena was playing well, and Iga seemed like she was out of answers. In the third set, as Jeļena raced away to a 3–6, 6–3, 6–1 victory, Iga was strangely accepting of her defeat.

"I really don't know what happened," she said. "I felt no control suddenly."[70]

Just like that, the defending US Open champion and Coco's biggest nemesis was out. It was officially Coco's tournament to win or lose. Team Coco was, of course, secretly a bit thrilled that she'd be playing Jeļena in the quarterfinals instead of running into Iga's revenge tour.

It was a good lesson that sports can be unpredictable, and you never know what's going to happen on a given day. Coco even teased the media that had been predicting for the last week that she would have to face Iga in the quarterfinals.

"I was shocked but also not shocked because I know the level that Jeļena can bring to the game," Coco said. "That's why you can never pay attention to what journalists say sometimes. No offense to you guys."[71]

The internal politics of scheduling the courts is always interesting during a Grand Slam. Every day, the tournament director sits down with a few members of their staff, looks at the matches that are coming up, and assigns them to a certain court and time depending on a few different factors, including what's best for television.

Because Coco was so popular and the TV people liked putting her on at night when more fans could watch, it seemed like a good bet that she'd play one of the late matches. That also seemed like the fair thing to do for Jeļena, who didn't get to bed until 5 a.m. after finishing the Iga match and going through her typical routine of cooldown and stretching in the gym, talking to the media, getting something to eat, and driving back to the hotel.

For that very reason, though, Coco's team was hoping for a daytime slot at Ashe, which would give Jeļena less time to recover. Plus, growing up in Florida made Coco used to playing in the kind of heat and humidity that was being forecast for quarterfinal day. Jeļena lives in Lativa, which is very cold for much of the year and almost never gets hot and sticky like New York in the summer.

"I can last as long as anybody in the women's side of the tournament, probably even some of the men," Coco said. "The heat means nothing to me."[72]

Predictably, Jeļena woke up feeling tired after the late night. Beating the number-one player in the world was a huge adrenaline rush and it was difficult to even go to sleep. The next day, her body caught up with her and it felt like one big sugar crash.

"I slept for, I don't know, maybe like seven or eight hours, but you don't completely recover," she said. "The whole day I felt very low energy."[73]

When Jeļena found out the US Open made her quarterfinal the very first match of the day, she was surprised and disappointed. The tournament seemed to be playing favorites by giving Coco the time slot she wanted, but that's life on the WTA Tour. The big star players, especially if they're Americans, tend to get the schedule they want at the US Open.

"I think it's a little bit crazy," she said. [74]

But there was nothing Jeļena could do about the circumstances. Coco was going to be more rested, and it was going to be very hot outside with the match starting at noon—both of which played in Coco's favor. Still, Team Coco had some concerns about the matchup, not just because of Jeļena's game style but because they had played earlier in the year at the Australian Open. Coco was supposed to win that match, too, but Jeļena had her A game that night and won pretty easily.

When the quarterfinal started, though, Jeļena wasn't the same player she had been against Iga or even against Coco in Australia. Some people can hide what they're feeling on the court because they don't want to show any weakness to their opponent. Jeļena isn't like that. You can tell how she's feeling at all times, often just by a facial expression. Whether it was being tired or the heat or still being mad about the scheduling situation, her slumped shoulders and eye rolls after almost every point she lost were showing the world she wasn't in the right mood to fight for her spot in the semifinals.

This was a match for Coco to keep the ball in the court and let Jeļena make the mistakes. At the same time, she couldn't get too comfortable because she was playing someone whose switch could flip on at any moment.

"Her timing or something wasn't working," Coco said. "I just told myself to stay on her."[75]

Coco made sure there was no letup. She punished Jeļena's sloppy, uninspired play with a 6–0 first set. By the second, Jeļena was arguing with her coaches, at one point even telling them she didn't want to play anymore. Jeļena finished the match, but she never gave herself a chance. In the quarterfinals of a Grand Slam, you expect a tough match. But this one was so one-sided, with Coco running away 6–2 in the second set, that she barely even celebrated on the court.

Still, it was a big moment for her. It was just the second time Coco had been in the semifinals of a Grand Slam and the first time a teenager from America had made it that far at the US Open since Serena. Coco felt especially honored by that.

"Being in any sentence with her is great," Coco said. "She's the greatest player of all time. I'm nothing close to that yet. She's my idol. I think if you told me when I was younger that I would be in these same stat lines as her, I would freak out."[76]

Coco always acknowledged the comparisons with Serena, but she didn't want to dwell on them. Especially at that time. A lot of people started the tournament wondering whether Coco could beat Iga again. As it turned out, good fortune was on her side and she had her easiest match of the tournament against a tired opponent. Things were lining up perfectly, but there was still more work to do.

***

Any time you put more than twenty-three thousand people in a stadium, there are going to be distractions. In a perfect world, they'd all be perfectly quiet and still during a match so that players could focus completely on the next point rather than something happening around them. But that's not how it works in real life. There's always going to be someone moving around looking for their seat or messing around with their phone or talking just a little too loud to the person next to them. Part of the mental strength it takes to win a Grand Slam is being able to block out all the noise and worry only about what you can control.

Every now and then, though, something happens that even the most experienced players and coaches don't know how to handle. And on semifinal night at the US Open, Coco found herself in the middle of a disruption that nobody in tennis had seen before.

The second set against Karolína Muchová had just begun, and things were going great for Coco. Karolína had been the more nervous player, and Coco was just steady enough to take a 6–4 lead. At that point in the match, Coco just wanted to keep it going the same direction. The last thing she needed was for something to happen that might knock her off rhythm or give Karolina a chance to regroup.

But as Karolína was getting ready to serve early in the second set, noise started coming from some seats way in the upper deck of the stadium. At first, it was hard to tell exactly what was going on, especially from the court level. But after a few seconds, everyone started to figure out that three people were standing up and chanting something that was difficult to hear in such a big stadium.

Pretty quickly, people in the stadium figured out they were protestors who came to the match for one reason: to disrupt it.

Over history, protestors have used sporting events as a way to draw attention to their cause. It can be annoying to the people playing and watching, but that's exactly the point. The protestors want to make sure you can't ignore them, even though what they're doing might be rude or inappropriate.

These particular protestors, wearing shirts that said "End Fossil Fuels," were affiliated with an environmental group that had actually snuck into several tennis tournaments during the year. One of them was Wimbledon, where the protestors threw confetti all over one of the courts and caused a slight delay as people cleaned it up.

In general, Coco was sympathetic to protestors. And this topic was one she cared about deeply as a young person who worries about what climate change is going to do to the planet when she's older. Coco had herself taken part in protests about racial injustice near her home in Florida. As a young Black woman from a family of teachers going back multiple generations, she understands that protest and civil disobedience has been part of American history since the very beginning and has a role to play in changing society for the better.

"I always speak about preaching what you feel and what you believe in," she said. "It was done in a peaceful way, so I can't get too mad at it. Obviously, I don't want it to happen when I'm winning 6–4, 1–0, and I wanted the momentum to keep going. But hey, if that's what they felt they needed to do to get their voices heard, I can't really get upset at it."[77]

The problem was, this wasn't a normal situation where the protestors make their point and get removed from their seats so that the match can continue. One of the men had somehow put glue all over his bare feet and stuck them to the concrete floor. The glue was so strong that when the security guards arrived, the man couldn't be removed. Getting him out was going to require special equipment and help from the police.

Inside the stadium, though, nobody could quite figure out what was going on and why it was taking so long to get the match started again. Fans started chanting, "Get them out! Get them out!" while Coco went to the corner to have a chat with her coaches and see if they had any information. Coach Brad shouted instructions as if the match was going to start up again at any second.

For a few minutes, Coco and Karolína just paced around the court to make sure their bodies didn't cool down if they were going to start playing again soon. But then, when more police arrived on the scene and it became obvious that this was going to be a long delay, they were told to go back to the locker room. Nobody knew when they might be able to play again.

Players are used to delays, but usually it's because of bad weather. Coco had never had to stop for this long because of somebody in the crowd—and in one of the most important matches of her life, no less. A lot of players in Coco's position would have been angry, especially because she was winning. This delay could have given Karolína an opportunity to collect her thoughts, calm down, and start playing better tennis.

"They told us it could be as quick as five minutes or as long as an hour," she said. "But, you know, it's life. It happens. I think I did a good job of staying focused."[78]

After fifty minutes, security was finally able to unglue the protestor's feet and restart the match, and Karolína had indeed settled her nerves. With each game, she was starting to play better. For Coco, who was hanging onto a slim 6–5 lead in the second set, the match didn't feel like it was even close to over. Many of the games had been going to deuce, and the rallies were getting longer and longer. Coco had to be mentally prepared to grind all the way to the last point because she knew that's what Karolína was going to do as well.

And the situation was starting to get urgent. Coco had let five match points escape her grasp, a couple of them with missed forehands. If she didn't win this game, the second set was going to be decided by a tiebreaker and the whole match would suddenly be up for grabs. It was crucial that she ended it right here.

Then, as she had done for the entire tournament, Coco won the point that mattered most—but it wasn't a match point. At yet another deuce, Coco and Karolina started to rally almost like they were on the practice court, both of them just trying to hit as many shots as possible without missing—back and forth, back and forth like a metronome on a piano.

"After ten or 15 shots in, I was, like, 'Well, this is going to change the match,'" Coco said.

Then fifteen shots became twenty, and twenty became thirty, neither player able to get the ball past the other. It was going to be the biggest point maybe of the entire tournament—and after forty shots and fifty-three seconds of rallying, Karolína finally blinked. Tired of hitting groundstroke after groundstroke, she tried to soften the hands and hit a drop shot that might catch Coco by surprise. It wasn't a bad idea, but Coco saw it immediately and sprinted toward the net. When the ball bounced, Coco was already there, waiting for with the whole court open in front of her to put away a forehand winner. She still had to win one more point, but with both of them now exhausted, that was the shot that decided the match.

"I knew that I could outlast that rally," Coco said. "I knew I had the legs and the lungs to outlast her in the rally; it was whether I had the mentality and patience to do it."[79]

A few moments later, Coco was in the US Open final, sealed with a spinning fist pump and a scream. The achievement brought back so many thoughts and memories and put into perspective just how far she had come in four years. When she looked back at herself in pictures and videos, from the carefree days as a fifteen-year-old to times when she left the court in tears after tough losses to the struggles she was having just a few weeks earlier to live up to her own expectations, it seemed like she was seeing a different person.

With what was about to be ahead of her in two days, though, Coco thought mostly about Kobe Bryant, one of her sporting icons. During the 2009 NBA Finals, he was asked by a reporter why he seemed unhappy after his team won game two. In the NBA, you need four to win a playoff series.

"What's there to be happy about? Job's not finished," he said.

Standing on the court addressing the celebrating crowd, Coco had the same thing in mind.

"Job's not done yet," she said.

CHAPTER 10

The little girl in the gray T shirt with pink-and-green sunglasses and her hair pulled back into a ballet bun was having the time of her life in the upper deck of Arthur Ashe Stadium. She was jumping around, hands in the air, and putting her hand to her ear like a phone as the Carly Rae Jensen song "Call Me Maybe" played over the loudspeakers.

It was Kids' Day at the US Open in 2012. Imagine going back in time and telling the people sitting all around that little girl, most of whom weren't even watching her dance, that eleven years later, she would be down on the court getting ready to play in the final. Would they have taken it seriously? Would she have even taken it seriously?

"That little girl, she had the dream," Coco said. "But I don't know if she fully believed it. As a kid, you have so many dreams. As you get older, sometimes it can fiddle away. I would tell her don't lose that dream."[80]

Somewhere along the journey, the purity of setting the highest goals and confidence to believe she could reach them faded away just a little bit. At fifteen, everything seemed possible for Coco. Then, life changed overnight—and not always for the better. People she didn't know wanted things from her all the time. People she would never meet or talk to had opinions about her tennis game, her looks, her family, her entire life.

In the moment, some of those challenges didn't make sense. They seemed like burdens that prevented Coco from doing what she wanted to do. But more recently, all of the pieces were starting to make sense. Yes, tennis was a job—and like all jobs, it had its highs and lows. There were going to be tough days. But if she took a step back and looked at the big picture, Coco was living an incredible life that allowed her to meet incredible people and play tennis in amazing places. Out of the millions and millions of girls who picked up a tennis racket, she had made it through her talent, hard work and passion from the public courts in Atlanta and Delray Beach to the top ten in the world. That was already an incredible achievement, even if she never won another match.

"I used to think negative things, like why is there so much pressure? Why is this so hard?" she said. "I realize in a way it's pressure, but it's not. There are people struggling to feed their families, people who don't know where their next meal is going to come from, people who have to pay their bills. That's real pressure, that's real hardship, that's real life. I'm in a very privileged position."[81]

After all the conversation during the year about her forehand and why she was losing in the early rounds of the Grand Slams, and her new coaching team and her parents, her turnaround really came down to the most basic thing.

Regardless of the result, she was enjoying this. She was living her dream. She was once again that eight-year-old girl dancing in Arthur Ashe Stadium. Only this time, she wasn't in the seats but rather in the locker room waiting to play Aryna Sabalenka, and she was about to go win a big silver trophy that would make her a Grand Slam champion forever. What would Coco tell herself now if she could go back in time to that Kids' Day when she saw endless possibilities for her life?

"I would just tell her just keep working and believing in that dream, and don't let the doubters diminish that," she said.[82]

In a couple hours, the doubters would be silent and the dream fulfilled.

***

There is always a strange vibe around the final days of a Grand Slam. By the semifinals and finals, the locker rooms and practice courts are almost empty. There aren't many fans roaming around the grounds. Compared to the first week of the tournament, it feels quiet and a little bit lonely. No matter how much players try to stick to their routines and treat the final like any other day, everyone feels the tension of being so close to the title. Even players who have won twenty or more Grand Slam titles admit that they get nervous. The question is always which player will be able to handle the nerves better on that day.

Corey Gauff had been nervous for pretty much the entire two weeks of the US Open, and Coco being in one close match after the other hadn't helped him stay calm. While her mom Candi had been in the players' box for every match sitting with Coach Brad, Coach Pere, and Coco's fitness trainer and hitting partner, nobody really knew where Corey was sitting.

Sometimes, he was spotted in one of the luxury boxes. Sometimes he was hopping from seat to seat. Sometimes, he was so stressed out he would get up and go pace around the concourse of the stadium. Wherever he was, Coco couldn't see him.

Of all the changes she had made this summer, that was the biggest one. No matter how many different coaches Coco worked with, her dad had always been in charge. He was the one who put a tennis racket in her hand, who encouraged her, who coached her, who followed her all over the world and protected her as she pursued greatness. Every night of the tournament, he was still giving Coco his scouting report on her opponents. But that's where his influence on her tennis now ended. For a lot of parents in similar situations, letting go and trusting others to get their kid over the last hurdle hasn't been so easy. But the quick success of Coco and her new coaches made it look like a great decision.

"He's the one who said, 'It's time for a new change, I can't do it anymore, so let's bring people in,'" Coco said.[83]

As a mature young woman now finding her way in the world as an adult, she was finally playing tennis for herself—not the money or the fame or because other people thought she could be the next Serena. But if there was one person she could win this last match for besides herself, it would be her dad. He was going to be in that big stadium somewhere, and even though Coco couldn't see him, his presence was everywhere.

Coco herself wasn't as nervous as she expected when she woke up on Saturday. The night before, she had been on the phone talking with friends until she finally fell asleep 1 a.m., but not much of the conversation was about tennis. If there was one thing Coco had learned from the French Open final the year before, it was to make sure none of those thoughts about winning or celebrating or holding the trophy even entered her mind.

"I think I wanted it too much," she said.

But there are always going to be thoughts swimming around your head before a match, and sometimes they're hard to control. As Coco waited and waited until it was time to finally get on the court, she pulled out her phone and made sure to read every post on social media from someone predicting her to lose.

"Some people need to shut off the comments on not look at them," she said. "But I'm an argumentative person. I'm very stubborn. Until ten minutes before the match, I was just reading comments of people saying I wasn't going to win. That just put the fire in me." [84]

What would the comments be like if Coco lost, though? For the first thirty-nine minutes of the final, that looked like a real possibility. Everyone in the stadium had shown up for a big New York party, and Aryna was spoiling it with her big, bad brand of power tennis. Just like against Laura Siegemund and Elise Mertens, Coco was going to have to come from behind.

Coach Brad didn't like what was seeing on the court, but he kept thinking about how similar this journey was to the ride he was on with Andre Agassi in 1999. Just like Coco, he kept getting in trouble and finding his way out of it. If Coco's destiny was to win this tournament, of course it was going to happen in the most difficult way possible.

"Maybe in years past, you get in that situation and you don't find your way out of it," Coach Brad said. "Sabalenka played a great first set and really took it to Coco. But the fact she'd been winning all summer gave me hope that it could change."

Another thing to consider was Aryna's state of mind. As big and tough as she looked on the court, with a large tattoo of a tiger's head etched into her left forearm, her history as a player was filled with missed opportunities and emotional breakdowns in big tournaments. The one exception was the Australian Open to start the year, when Aryna had the best night of her life in the final. But in many other big matches that she had played in the US Open, Wimbledon, and the French Open, Aryna's high-risk game broke down when the opportunity to win was right in front of her nose. The battle for Aryna is always more emotional than physical. If things get tense, she struggles to relax. Her body's response is to hit with even more power and aim even closer to the lines, which usually backfires because she'll miss more and get angrier with herself and the situation.

"It's me against me," she said.[85]

As the old saying goes, tigers can't change their stripes. But it was going to be up to Coco—and the crowd—to change the momentum of the match.

If Coach Brad could pick one moment where things turned in Coco's favor, it was at 1–1 in the second set. Coco was serving, trying whatever she could to put some pressure on Aryna, but starting the game with a double fault wasn't the answer. The crowd groaned. Coco rolled her eyes in disgust. Coach Brad sat with his elbows on his knees, leaning forward with his hands clasped together in front of his mouth. Coco needed to respond right now.

Like so many times during her winning streak, everything good started with the serve. A 118-mile-per-hour rocket handcuffed Aryna, and she couldn't put it in play. Back to 15–15. Then another one, just as hard and effective, for 30–15. Coco's serve hadn't really made an impact in this match yet, but then she fired a clean ace on the next point for 40–15. And to close out the game at 40–30, Coco fired yet another first serve into Aryna's forehand that was too fast to return.

"Come onnnnnnnn!" she screamed.

It was the first time all day something looked easy for Coco. A statement had been made. The fans, who had been quiet as Aryna dominated the first set, had a reason to get fired up again.

"That game got Coco going, and it got the crowd going and they never relaxed," Coach Brad said. "The crowd was awesome, and Coco really needed them."

***

An hour and ten minutes later, Coco had arrived at championship point. After experiencing the lowest point in her career two months earlier and wondering whether she had what it took to win a Grand Slam—almost learning to being at peace with herself if it never happened—she finally realized she was actually about to win it.

Coco knew it. Coach Brad knew it. Everyone in the stadium, including her mom and dad, knew it. And Aryna knew it, too, because she had been completely outplayed by this phenomenal nineteen-year-old on the biggest stage in the sport.

Coco almost won the final point with another ace sliding away from Aryna's forehand, but she lunged just in time to get her racket on it. Coco played two safe crosscourt backhands to get the rally started, then rolled a forehand high over the net that Aryna jumped forward to hit hard, with her momentum carrying her toward the net.

The ball came back to Coco's forehand, and she quickly chose to hit it down the line, hoping it would catch Aryna a little bit flat-footed since the crosscourt shot is the one players will hit more often in that situation. It worked to perfection. Aryna had to scoot to her left and jump off the ground to hit a high backhand volley, which is one of the most difficult shots in tennis to control.

Suddenly, this was it. This was Coco's shot to end it. As Aryna's volley bounced high off the court, Coco saw a huge opening on the left side of the net to scoop a little backhand that Aryna wouldn't have enough time to reach. As the ball floated past Aryna, Coco dropped her racket and fell backward into the concrete of Arthur Ashe Stadium. She was now the US Open champion.

The minutes that followed were maybe the most emotional in her entire tennis career. After a few seconds of shock as she lay on the ground, Coco got up and walked toward the net, where Aryna was waiting to give her a congratulatory hug. Then, she put her knees on the ground and the tears began to flow as she raised her racket to acknowledge the fans.

Finally, she ran to the corner of the stadium and was guided by security through about rows of seats until she saw someone special waiting for her: Corey.

For twenty or twenty-five seconds, they embraced and wouldn't let each other go. Then Coco noticed something she had never seen before: he was crying. They both were.

"My parents and my dad dream big, and he was wearing a shirt today that said 'Imagine,'" Coco said. "He showed me that imaginations can come true. It's not always just the image in your head. You can make it a reality."[86]

Corey and Candi Gauff had done everything right. They knew when to push. They knew when to step back. They sacrificed their own careers to give their daughter every possible chance to become a champion. But most of all, they had done their best to make sure that Coco's life and self-image wasn't completely wrapped up in tennis.

As she admitted, it had been a struggle to find that balance growing from a fifteen-year-old who became an instant superstar into a nineteen-year-old professional who was not yet fulfilling her potential. But now Coco had arrived as a Grand Slam champion, and the best part was that it wasn't going to change the most important things about her. Tennis, as Candi would often remind her, is what she does. It's not who she is.

"In the past, when I would lose, I would think I was not worth it as a person," Coco said. "My parents always reminded me that they loved me regardless how I do. I think that helped me today because I realize regardless if I came home with this trophy or not, I'm still a person and I still do a lot of good in this world outside of the court."[87]

But having the trophy was pretty nice, too. It was a reward for all the work she had put in and all the losses she had taken and all the growth she had embraced over the past year. In that moment, reflecting on everything it took to get where she was right at that moment, Coco wished that just for a second she could go back in time and hand that trophy to her eight-year old self as a promise for what was going to happen in her life.

Coco would want that little girl to know there would be plenty of challenges and even some sadness along the way. But as a US Open champion for the rest of her life, she'd know that every one of those tears would be worth it.

ENDNOTES

1   Coco Gauff, 2023 US Open press conference,
    Queens, New York, September 9, 2023.

2   Ibid.

3   Aryna Sabalenka 2023 US Open press conference,
    Queens, New York, September 9, 2023.

4   Roger Federer, 2017 Wimbledon press conference,
    London, England, July 14, 2017.

5   Greg Garber, "Why 12-Year-Old Cori Gauff
    Hopes She'll Be the Greatest of All Time,"
    ESPN, January 3, 2017, https://www.
    espn.com/tennis/story/_/id/18401434/
    tennis-why-12-year-old-cori-gauff-thinks-greatest-all.

6   Venus Williams, 2019 Wimbledon press conference,
    London, England, July 1, 2019.

7   Gauff, 2023 US Open press conference, Queens, New York, September 9, 2023.

8   Gauff, 2023 Western & Southern Open press conference, Mason, Ohio, August 19, 2023.

9   Paul Newman, "Wimbledon Winner Petra Kvitova Learns to Live with Her Celebrity Status," *Independent*, October 15, 2014, https://www.independent.co.uk/sport/tennis/wimbledon-winner-petra-kvitova-learns-to-live-with-her-celebrity-status-9797041.html.

10   Sloane Stephens, 2021 US Open press conference, Queens, New York, August 30, 2021.

11   Gauff, 2023 US Open press conference, Queens, New York, August 25, 2023.

12   Alyssa Roenigk, "Coco Gauff Is Ready for Greatness, on Her Own Terms," ESPN, August 23, 2022, https://www.espn.com/tennis/story/_/id/34424448/coco-gauff-ready-greatness-own-terms.

13   Coco Gauff, 2022 US Open press conference, Queens, New York, August 26, 2022.

14   Ibid.

15   Venus Williams, "Wimbledon has sent me a message: I'm only a second class champion." The Times.co.uk. June 26, 2023. https://www.thetimes.co.uk/article/

wimbledon-has-sent-me-a-message-im-only-a-second-class-champion-f056h05hmzq

16 Venus Williams, "Champions of Equality: Standing Up for What's Right," US Open.com, September 7, 2023, https://www.usopen.org/en_US/news/articles/2023-09-07/champions_of_equality_standing_up_for_whats_right.html.

17 Serena Williams, 2019 Wimbledon press conference, London, England, June 29, 2019.

18 Gauff, 2019 Wimbledon press conference, London, England, July 1, 2019.

19 Ibid.

20 Ibid.

21 Federer, 2019 Wimbledon press conference, London, England, July 2, 2019.

22 Gauff, 2019 Wimbledon press conference, London, England, July 3, 2019.

23 Gauff, 2019 Wimbledon press conference, London, England, July 5, 2019.

24 Gauff, 2019 Wimbledon press conference, London, England, July 8, 2019.

25 Simona Halep, 2019 Wimbledon press conference, London, England, July 8, 2019.

26 Gauff, 2022 Roland Garros press conference, Paris, France, May 22, 2022.

27 Ibid.

28 Patrick Snell and Sam Joseph, "Coco Gauff: Even at the Age of 10, Tennis Coach Patrick Mouratoglou Was Convinced US Star Would Be 'Great,'" CNN, September 23, 2023, https://www.cnn.com/2023/09/23/sport/coco-gauff-serena-williams-tennis-coach-spt-intl/index.html.

29 Gauff, 2022 Roland Garros press conference, Paris, France, May 25, 2022.

30 Arthur Kapetanakis, "Anisimova Tops Gauff in All-U.S. Junior US Open Final," USTA, September 10, 2017, https://www.usta.com/en/home/stay-current/national/anisimova-tops-gauff-in-all-american-us-open-girls--final.html#tab=tournaments.

31 Gauff, "Coco Gauff," April 14, 2020, https://behindtheracquet.com/coco-gauff/.

32 United States Tennis Association "Cori Gauff Reflects on Winning 2018 Roland Garros Girls' Singles Title," YouTube video, 3:26, June 9, 2018, https://www.youtube.com/watch?v=sRg3RmuGIxg&t=70s.

33 Gauff, 2022 Roland Garros press conference, Paris, France, May 27, 2022.

34 Gauff, 2022 Roland Garros press conference, Paris, France, May 31, 2022.

35 Gauff, 2022 Roland Garros press conference, Paris, France, June 4, 2022.

36 Gauff press conference, 2023 US Open press conference, Queens, New York, September 9, 2023.

37 Gauff, 2022 Adelaide International press conference, Adelaide, Australia, January 4, 2022.

38 Gauff, WTA Finals press conference, Fort Worth, Texas, October 29, 2022.

39 Paula Badosa, Matua Madrid Open press conference, Madrid, Spain, April 29, 2023.

40 Gauff, 2023 Roland Garros press conference, Paris, France May 26, 2023.

41 Gauff, 2023 Rothesay International press conference, Eastbourne, England, June 29, 2023.

42 Gauff, 2023 Roland Garros press conference Paris, France, May 26, 2023.

43 Gauff, 2023 Roland Garros press conference, Paris, France, June 7, 2023.

44 Gauff, 2023 Wimbledon press conference, London, England, July 3, 2023.

45 Gauff, 2023 US Open press conference, Queens, New York, September 9, 2023.

46 Gauff, 2023 US Open press conference, Queens, New York, September 3, 2023.

47 Gauff, 2023 US Open press conference, Queens, New York, September 5, 2023.

48 Gauff, 2023 Mubadala DC Citi Open press conference, Washington, D.C., August 6, 2023.

49 Ibid.

50 Ibid.

51 Ibid.

52 Gauff, 2023 Omnium Banque Nationale press conference, Montreal, Canada, August 11, 2023.

53 Gauff, Western & Southern Open press conference, Cincinnati, Ohio, August 20, 2023.

54 Gauff, 2023US Open press conference, Queens, New York, August 28, 2023.

55 Ibid.

56 Ibid.

57 Ibid.

58 Laura Siegemund, 2023 US Open press conference, Queens, New York, August 28, 2023.

59 Ibid.

60 Ibid.

61 Gauff, 2023 US Open press conference, Queens, New York, August 28, 2023.

62 Ibid.

63 Gauff, 2023 US Open press conference, Queens, New York, August 30, 2023.

64 Gauff, 2023 US Open press conference, Queens, New York, September 1, 2023.

65 Caroline Wozniacki, 2023 US Open press conference, Queens, New York, September 1, 2023.

66 Gauff, 2023 US Open press conference, Queens, New York, September 1, 2023.

67 Gauff, 2023 US Open press conference, Queens, New York, September 3, 2023.

68 Ibid.

69 Ibid.

70 Iga Świątek, 2023 US Open press conference, Queens, New York, September 4, 2023.

71 Gauff, 2023 US Open press conference, Queens, New York, September 5, 2023.

72 Gauff, 2023 US Open press conference, Queens, New York, September 9, 2023.

73 Jeļena Ostapenko, 2023 US Open press conference, Queens, New York, September 5, 2023.

74 Ibid.

75 Gauff, 2023 US Open press conference, Queens, New York, September 5, 2023.

76 Ibid.

77 Gauff, 2023 US Open press conference, Queens, New York, September 7, 2023.

78 Ibid.

79 Ibid.

80 Gauff, 2023 US Open press conference, Queens, New York, September 9, 2023.

81 Gauff, 2023 US Open press conference, Queens, New York, September 5, 2023.

82 Gauff, 2023 US Open press conference, Queens, New York, September 9, 2023.

83 Gauff, television interview, ESPN, Queens, New York, September 9, 2023.

84 Gauff, 2023 US Open press conference, Queens, New York, September 9, 2023.

85 Aryna Sabalenka, 2023 US Open press conference, Queens, New York, September 9, 2023.

86 Gauff, 2023 US Open press conference, Queens, New York, September 9, 2023.

87 Ibid.

ABOUT THE AUTHOR

D an Wolken is an award-winning columnist for *USA TODAY Sports* who has spent more than two decades primarily covering college sports, the NBA, the Olympic Games, tennis, and horse racing. His work has been recognized multiple times by the Associated Press Sports Editors. Prior to *USA TODAY*, Wolken's work appeared on FOX Sports and in *The Commercial Appeal*, where he primarily wrote about the Memphis Tigers' basketball program during its rise to the Final Four under John Calipari. A 2001 graduate of Vanderbilt University, Wolken started his career at Colorado Springs's *The Gazette*. He currently lives in Atlanta, Georgia and plays tennis every chance he gets.